THE GOSPEL IN HARD TIMES

Joni and Friends
Pat Verbal

STUDY GUIDE with LEADER'S NOTES

New
Growth
Press
WWW.NEWGROWTHPRESS.COM

New Growth Press, Greensboro, NC 27404
www.newgrowthpress.com
Copyright © 2019 by Joni and Friends

Cover Design: Faceout Books, faceoutstudios.com
Interior Typesetting and eBook: lparnellbookservices.com
Writer: Pat Verbal
Editor: Chonda Ralston

ISBN 978-1-948130-72-1 (print)
ISBN 978-1-948130-80-6 (ebook)

Printed in the United States of America

27 26 25 24 23 22 21 20 19   1 2 3 4 5

CONTENTS

FOREWORD FROM JONI

What brings you to a Bible study with "Hard Times" in the title? Divorce, disease, a financial crisis with no relief in sight? Perhaps your life has been altered by disability, like mine, or maybe you are here as support for a friend going through a difficult season? Regardless of what brought you here, I can assure you that you're in the right place.

I'm Joni Eareckson Tada. After I broke my neck in a diving accident at seventeen, I faced many of the same questions you may have: *Why me, God? How can such tragedies be part of your plan?* Looking back on more than fifty years as a quadriplegic in a wheelchair, having endured chronic pain, as well as a battle with breast cancer, I can assure you that God isn't afraid of our questions. In fact, he wants us to cry out—scream out to him if we must—because when we turn to God and his Word for answers, we'll find a loving Father who promises to never let us out of his sight and who wants to turn our tragedies into triumphs.

C. S. Lewis once wrote, "God whispers to us in our pleasures, speaks in our conscience, but shouts in our pain: it is His megaphone to rouse a deaf world."[1] When we trust God through life's hardships and struggles, we find our own faith strengthened—and our friends and neighbors notice. When the church rallies around those in need and becomes a safe place to find hope and healing, the world takes notice. My prayer is that this study will start that awakening within you and within your congregation.

As a restless teenager watching my friends leave for college while I learned to navigate life with limited mobility, I couldn't have known that God would call me to start an international disability ministry and travel the world as an advocate on behalf of those affected by disability. What might God want to do as you trust him with your struggles?

Let's seek him and find out.

INTRODUCTION

Hard times come to every human being in various forms, degrees, and stages of life. We live in a broken world, so we all suffer for all kinds of reasons—poverty, disease, disability, loss, broken relationships—the list is as long and unique as each of our circumstances. We can't really compare our hard times to others, but we can be assured that God knows all about what we are experiencing and will not leave us or forsake us.

Suffering is a catalyst that can deepen our understanding of God's plan. How we choose to react to hardship has life-altering potential. Conflict and pain force us beyond our comfort zone to seek answers. We seemingly understand this better on a physical level than in the spiritual realm. For example, we take vitamins for a weak body, seek education to improve our minds, go to physical therapy for aching joints, or join a dating website for a lonely heart. While these efforts are useful, hard times usually bring us to a spiritual fork in the road as well. We ignore this truth at our own peril.

Augustine of Hippo said, "Thou has made us for thyself, and our heart is restless until it finds its rest in thee." Herein lies the good news of the gospel. Regardless of the source or duration of our hardships in a broken world, God has created us for his glory. And Jesus, in his death and resurrection, has opened the door to the forgiveness, restoration, relationship, and the assurance of eternal life.

In this small group Bible study, we'll look to Jesus, our Great Shepherd, for answers to today's hard questions. Why am I going through this? Where is God when I need him? Can the church help me carry this burden? We'll discover how a diverse faith community—"one body with many parts"—can not only meet our needs but help us reach out to those in society who are afflicted and marginalized. The church holds the healing and hope the world needs. Regardless of current circumstances, we can boast in our afflictions because we know Christ's power rests in us.

"That's why I take pleasure in my weaknesses, and in the insults, hardships, persecutions, and troubles that I suffer for Christ. For when I am weak, then I am strong" (2 Corinthians 12:10 NLT).

The gospel works—especially in hard times.

ABOUT THIS STUDY

The Gospel in Hard Times is a small group study intended to help you understand the presence and power of God in the midst of life's hardships and struggles. God wants to redeem every situation and use it to deepen your faith and make you more like Jesus Christ. In these lessons, you will meet real-life people in crisis—ordinary people in a sea of hopelessness who have watched God turn their darkness into light.

There are eight lessons. Each lesson is self-contained, featuring clear teaching from Scripture, and requires no extra work outside of the group setting. You will have optional ways to keep applying what you've learned between lessons, but you will be able to fully participate in each group meeting whether or not you've done the optional activities.

LESSON 1: HARD TIMES, HARD QUESTIONS

Hard times are part of the human condition. They come in various forms, degrees, and life stages to both the innocent and the guilty.

Some struggles originate from false beliefs, misguided choices, or selfish behaviors, and others seem arbitrary. But none of our troubles surprise God. In John 16:33 Jesus warned his followers, "In the world you will have tribulation. But take heart; I have overcome the world." As believers, we face a choice: Will I allow suffering to overwhelm me and drive me away from God? Or will I cry out to God in my distress and come to Christ, the overcomer?

LESSON 2: JESUS IDENTIFIES WITH OUR SORROW

In this lesson, we see Jesus as our fellow-sufferer who identifies with all our struggles. Isaiah 53:3 says, "He was despised and rejected by men; a man of sorrows, and acquainted with grief." It is natural to wonder why God allowed his Son to endure such affliction and pain. But Jesus suffered willingly on the cross to become "the source of eternal salvation to all who obey him" (Hebrews 5:9). So in your loneliest, darkest hour, you can rest assured that Jesus understands, cares, and has a plan of redemption.

LESSON 3: AN EVER-PRESENT HELP

In this lesson, we'll consider how our Good Shepherd knows the way through life's valleys. While we tend to give in to sadness and isolation, the Good Shepherd is always beside us, prodding us to higher ground. He never forgets or abandons his own. He knows his sheep and leads each one to new strengths in difficult seasons. As we follow Jesus, we remember his gentle faithfulness and give thanks in every circumstance.

LESSON 4: A PLACE OF HEALING

In this lesson, we examine God's call to lay down our heavy burdens and remove the masks that prevent us from living authentic lives. Whether we face chronic pain, mental disorders, broken relationships, or isolation due to a disability, suffering can prevent us from fully participating in life, as well as in the family of God. Only as we embrace the biblical meaning of healing can we comfort others and transform our churches into places of healing and hope.

LESSON 5: BRING IN THE BROKEN

In this lesson, we discover that God's mission for the church includes all people, especially those who are treated unjustly by society. In Jesus's time on earth, he often stopped to help the sick, poor, and disabled. In Luke 14:12–24, he used a parable to give his followers a powerful mandate about welcoming and including people who are marginalized and disabled into the life of the church.

LESSON 6: ONE BODY, MANY PARTS

In this lesson, we focus on making disciples of all who believe in Jesus Christ. People who are disabled and marginalized often feel they have nothing to offer or they don't belong—even in the church. But God's spiritual gifts are for all people, without exception and regardless of abilities. In 1 Corinthians 12:22 the apostle Paul describes the church as one body with many parts. He goes a step further saying the church is incomplete when it fails to include those "parts of the body that seem weakest and least important [because they] are actually the most necessary" (NLT).

LESSON 7: LIVING FOR CHRIST: JONI'S STORY

In this lesson, we consider how we can honor God and serve others through our suffering. We've all read about people who have faced unimaginable affliction and pain but somehow continue to remain steadfast in their Christian faith. Over the past few lessons, we've learned that no one is immune from suffering in our world. We've also seen how God can redeem our struggles for his purposes. Joni Eareckson Tada has triumphed through tremendous adversity for more than fifty years by trusting in God's redemptive plan and believing that his incredible power rests upon her.

LESSON 8: REASONS FOR HOPE

In this lesson, we celebrate our hope in Jesus Christ who died in our place and swung open the door to spiritual healing and eternal life. This is the good news of the gospel. Regardless of our abilities, fears, or weaknesses, our hope must be in "the living God, who is the Savior of all people, especially of those who believe" (1 Timothy 4:10). Even when our prayers seem to go unanswered, we can trust that God is working all things together for our good (see Romans 8:28).

HOW TO USE THIS STUDY

Each lesson follows a similar format, beginning with a quote and a promise statement that prepare your thinking, and with a summary of the lesson to come. From there, the lesson includes the following elements:

HARD TIMES IN THE WORLD

These articles begin with original stories that show we're not alone in our struggles. Whether problems are physical, emotional, or intellectual, you will meet men and women with whom you can identify and relate to their suffering and their victories. The articles will show how we, according to God's plan, live in a world and a time of many struggles. Acknowledging this will prepare us for the Bible discussion that follows. You will usually read through this article on your own, with a chance to discuss your thoughts with the group when you're done, unless your group prefers to have someone read it aloud.

BIBLE FOUNDATION

In this section, you will read along with your group and study together what the Bible says about the lesson topic, applying it through exercises and discussions. Relevant Scripture passages will provide direct insights using biblical characters that illustrate the lesson.

THE WITNESS

Just as Jesus taught through story, video can be an effective tool for many learners. The video clips provided from the *Joni and Friends* television series feature real-life testimonies that illustrate the biblical teaching and lesson objectives. As Joni Eareckson Tada likes to say, "These episodes are about friends who have changed my life."

PRAYER FOCUS

It's important to plan for prayer time at the beginning of the lesson. Prayer may be the most crucial part of your time together. You can use the suggested prayer focus or feel free to pray about specific needs expressed in your group discussions. Close with a reminder to continue praying for one another throughout the week in anticipation of your next session together.

ACTION PLAN

There is a tried-and-true teaching philosophy that says: Tell me, I forget. Show me, I remember. Involve me, I understand. The action plans are designed to apply God's Word between lessons, in ways that transform our actions and keep us in touch with what we've learned. Some reinforce regular practices, while others can help establish new habits. We encourage group members to share their experiences with the previous week's plan.

1

HARD TIMES, HARD QUESTIONS

*Our Father works a most kind good
through our most grievous losses.*
—DAVID POWLISON[1]

TAKEAWAY:

God wants to bring good from our suffering
as we lean into him and trust him with the results.

Hard times are part of the human condition. They come in various forms, degrees, and life stages to both the innocent and the guilty. Some struggles originate from false beliefs, misguided choices, or selfish behaviors, and others seem arbitrary. But none of our troubles surprise God. In John 16:33 Jesus warned his followers, "In the world you will have tribulation. But take heart; I have overcome the world." As believers, we face a choice: Will I allow suffering to overwhelm me and drive me away from God? Or will I cry out to God in my distress and come to Christ, the overcomer?

* * * *

On your own, read the article below until you get to the reflection questions. Think about your answers, or write them down. When everyone is ready, share some of your thoughts with the group if you're comfortable doing so.

"Should we accept only good things from the hand of God and never anything bad?" (Job 2:10 NLT).

Lesson

**HARD TIMES
IN THE
WORLD**

Facing the Unimaginable

Michael Hoggatt, a special educator and social worker, and his wife Mandy adopted their daughter Summer, knowing she had lived in nine foster homes before the age of three. They knew Summer had some intellectual and physical disabilities but were unaware she had suffered sexual abuse. In the midst of juggling her multiple services, Summer's behavior and anger haunted Michael. He began to question his role as her father and blamed himself. He wondered if they were the right "forever family" for her. Then, the unimaginable happened.

A few days after Summer's fifth birthday, she started bleeding. After months of tests, the doctor said Summer's kidney showed stage-four cancer, which could prove fatal. Mandy and Michael were in shock as they rushed Summer to the hospital. Suddenly their worries over her behavior seemed insignificant. The night before surgery, Michael drove home at 2:00 a.m. to pick up some things. David Crowder's song, "How He Loves," played on the car radio.[2] It reminded Michael how God's love for him was weighty and powerful, like a hurricane full of mercy.

Michael pulled off the freeway, unable to see through his tears. At that moment, he didn't ask God to fix Summer's disabilities; he begged

God to help Summer through the surgery and give him another day with her. Michael realized how much he wanted his daughter— not the child she could be, but his little girl, disabilities, anger, and all. God was faithful. Two years later, Summer was cancer-free and enjoying her real forever family.[3]

WHY, GOD, WHY?

Why did a young mother's legs have to be amputated after the bombing at the Boston Marathon? Why did a gunman open fire in a Charleston church one June evening killing nine innocent people? Why are forty-three young children diagnosed with cancer every day in America?[4] Why was a mom saved alone while nine members of her family drowned when a tourist boat capsized in Branson, Missouri?

These tragedies make no sense to us. Attempts to explain them frequently lead to conflicting views about how God works in the world. For example, Rabbi Harold S. Kushner's popular book, *When Bad Things Happen to Good People*, describes God as a bystander who neither causes nor participates in any tragedy we might face. God's only role is to come alongside us after the fact, according to Kushner. If this were true, how can we call God the Sovereign Ruler of the universe? Other contemporary authors such as Richard Dawkins and Christopher Hitchens (known atheists) pit the scientific community against Christianity, declaring war on the very existence of God. Such suppositions are in conflict with the truths in God's Word.

While Christians should be mindful of useful medical and scientific advances, we must remember whose we are and what we believe. It's okay to wrestle with God's truth, knowing he welcomes our questions.

Why can't I pay my monthly bills when I'm working two jobs?

Why does my son get bullied at school over his learning disabilities?

Why can't my grandma remember my name anymore?

Why this? Why now? Why me?

The Bible tells us God knows what he is doing even when we can't understand it. He "works all things according to the counsel of his will" (Ephesians 1:11).

> Oh, the depth of the riches and wisdom and knowledge of God! How unsearchable are his judgments and how inscrutable his ways!
> "For who has known the mind of the Lord,
>   or who had been his counselor?"
> "Or who has given a gift to him
>   that he might be repaid?"
> For from him and through him and to him are all things. To him be glory forever. Amen. (Romans 11:33–36)

God is involved in our pre-suffering and post-suffering, as well as being present in all the circumstances of our lives. No one is immune to the effects of living in a fallen, broken world.

At some point, most of us will experience one or all of the four basic kinds of suffering:

- **Physical suffering** can include bodily pain and discomfort, as well as cognitive and mental health issues.
- **Spiritual suffering** is a consequence of sin and separation from God.
- **Emotional suffering** is brought on by life circumstances such as heartbreak, divorce, loss of a loved one, and other disappointments.
- **Social and/or cultural suffering** involves religious rejection, economic exclusion, social segregation, and/or political discrimination.

Suffering is a great equalizer, but the degree and duration of our pain may be very different. Some experiences are lifelong; others can be a one-time crisis with a beginning and an end. In all of them, however, we have God's promise to sustain us: "For I know the plans I have for you, declares the LORD, plans for welfare and not for evil, to give you a future and a hope" (Jeremiah 29:11).

REFLECTION QUESTIONS:

What areas of hardship are you dealing with today—a hard season of parenting, a marriage on the verge of collapse, financial struggles, or a health crisis?

Have your hardships tended to pull you away from God or draw you closer to him? How?

After sharing some responses, have someone read aloud as you complete the rest of the lesson together, or take turns reading.

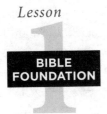

BIBLE FOUNDATION

Our God Is Steadfast, Not Heartless

If you have experienced suffering of any kind, you are in good company. Throughout Scripture, we see God using disability and hardship in the lives of his people to accomplish his purposes. Hannah grieved over infertility (1 Samuel 1:10–11). Moses had a speech problem (Exodus 4:10). Joseph endured slavery and later languished in prison for years even though he was an innocent man (Genesis 37:28; 39:20). Paul experienced a "thorn in his flesh" which some believe affected his vision (2 Corinthians 12:7). God's prophets promised a future to those who have suffered yet remained faithful (Micah 4:6–7; Zephaniah 3:19).

The life of Job helps us gain a renewed perspective on how to trust God in hard times, knowing that even the worst suffering has first been sifted through his hands. Dr. Larry Waters taught extensively on the life of Job, and offers this overview: "The book of Job is a mixture of divine and human wisdom which addresses a major life-issue: why righteous people suffer undeservedly. It shows that the sufferer can question and doubt, face hard questions of life with faith, maintain an unbroken relationship with God, and still come to a satisfactory resolution for personal and collective injustice and undeserved suffering."[5]

We see all four basic kinds of suffering revealed through Job: physical, spiritual, emotional, and social. Look up the passages below and identify the kind of suffering exemplified in each verse.

Job 12:4 _____ *SOCIAL* _____

Job 2:7–8, 12 _____ *PHYSICAL* _____

Job 23:8–9, 15 _____ *SPIRITUAL* _____

Job 7:4, 13–14 _____

How is it possible that such a good, God-fearing man like Job suffered so much? How was he able to continue to trust God? Instead of providing straightforward answers to hard questions, God showed himself to be a glorious, all-knowing, and almighty God (Job 38–41). During it all, Job proclaimed his faith: "For I know that my Redeemer lives, and at the last he will stand upon the earth" (Job 19:25).

Throughout Job's season of great sorrow and suffering, he discovered three truths about godly wisdom.

1. We cannot always count on truth from those around us.
2. God knows the way to wisdom because it resides in him alone.
3. Human beings can only find ultimate wisdom in a relationship with God.

"God understands the way to [wisdom], and he knows its place. For he looks to the ends of the earth and sees everything under the heavens" (Job 28:23–24).

DISCUSSION QUESTIONS:

- Since the answers to hardship are in your relationship with God, how are you developing that relationship?
- What could you do to develop it further?

Lesson

THE WITNESS

Good Can Come Out of Hard Times

Nick Vujicic is a people person and a hugger, which is incredible since he has no arms. Nick travels the world speaking to millions, which is astounding because he has no legs. He is also an author, worldwide evangelist, husband, father, and founder of Life Without Limbs (www.LifeWithoutLimbs.org).

Nick's disability gives him a platform to share new hope for whatever situations his audiences face. Just as God has used Nick to draw people to himself, he can use all believers to tell the gospel story.

Watch a clip from Nick's story (Video One at joniandfriends.org/gospel-hard-times). Then discuss the questions below.

DISCUSSION QUESTIONS:

- How does God bring good out of Nick's circumstances?
- How do you see yourself in Nick's story, and what are you willing to do to let God use you to draw attention to himself?

In the video, Nick shared that he lived with an *if only* mindset for years until he realized that God wanted to use his struggles to help others find joy in spite of their circumstances. Like the apostle Paul who wrote, "In all these things we are more than conquerors through him who loved us" (Romans 8:37), Nick has learned what it takes to find victory through hard times.

> When you can put your faith in God's grace, in God's plan for you, even when you don't understand, that's more than a conqueror. A conqueror is someone who defeats and overcomes a circumstance. But more than a conqueror is already having victory over something that's still there in your life as a circumstance and you didn't have to do a thing. It's that change of the Holy Spirit that comes in your heart that gives you that ability and transformation as more than a conqueror.

Like Nick, Joni Eareckson Tada had questions about how to live with her disabilities. She too discovered the answer was part of trusting God with her imperfections.

> When we wonder why we suffer, we are asking a question of someone. That someone is God. Why he created suffering doesn't matter as much as how we respond. When we can't find answers, we can find peace in the simple truth that we need him. After years of suffering, I've concluded that God uses suffering like a sandblasting machine stripping away our anxiety, complaints, and "I don't care" attitudes. Our afflictions rip away these things so we can see others with the eyes of Christ. When our hearts hurt, God feels that pain first. Suffering strengthens our souls and helps us know him better. And as we do, we become less "me" focused, and more God-focused.[6]

In hard times, we each face a choice. Will we listen to the critical voices, those outside and within? Or will we choose to believe what God says? Job chose to listen to God's voice, not the voice of Satan or others. Job 42:5 records how suffering deepened his relationship with God: "I had heard of you by the hearing of the ear, but now my eye sees you."

In the next lesson, we'll discover how God the Son endured suffering of every kind here on earth. In this way, Jesus Christ became our fellow-sufferer who identifies with all of our struggles.

> For it has been granted to you that for the sake of Christ you should not only believe in him, but also suffer for his sake. (Philippians 1:29)

Lesson

PRAYER FOCUS

Consider making the following items part of your closing prayer time together or part of your personal prayers in the coming week:

- Lord, thank you for the love letters in your Word that bring me peace, even when I don't understand.
- Lord, use me to weep with those who weep (Romans 12:15). I'm willing to befriend others through their grief. Keep me alert to recognize their needs and bold enough to share my faith journey.
- Lord, thank you for these friends who support me and pray for me. (List their names below.)

Use the action plan below to stay involved with what you have learned, on your own, until the next time the group meets. You will have a chance to discuss it at that meeting.

Lesson

ACTION PLAN

Grief Recovery

Have you noticed that the more you feed a problem, the bigger it gets? Our emotions can become so overbearing that they block our vision, crush our good intentions, and drain our energy. Emotions, however, are much like pain receptors for the body. They sometimes serve as God-given indicators that something is wrong. In seasons of crisis and sorrow, we tend to stuff our emotions, hiding our feelings from others—even God. When this happens, we need a plan that can lead us through our grief.

Are you currently experiencing anxiety and stress over a situation that seems out of your control? Have you prayed about it repeatedly without getting an answer? If so, you may be stuck on one or more of these stages of grief recovery.

NOTE: Grief is very personal. It's not merely for end-of-life issues. It can include any life-changing situation: medical diagnoses, injury, job loss, divorce, chronic pain, and many others. The steps to recovery can move forward or backward over different periods of time.[7] This is an introduction to the grief recovery process. To learn more, visit the Biblical Counseling Coalition at biblicalcounselingcoalition.org (see endnote for reference for a Christian perspective on the stages of grief).

1. **Denial** – "I can't believe this is happening to me." Denial is an initial stage of confusion that comes when we get bad news. It can also be a valuable form of self-protection.

2. **Anger** – "I see what is happening, and I'm really mad about it." Anger is a natural response to helplessness. It can be directed inward or toward God and others. Yet, a healthy amount of anger and fear can be good because it motivates us to consider our options.

3. **Bargaining** – "I'll do anything I can to make it stop." In this stage, we try to change the situation ourselves by bargaining with God, rather than trusting his divine will.

4. **Depression** – "I'm very sad because I realize I can't change my situation." Depression is a period of hopelessness. With God's help, it can lead to a more honest evaluation of the situation, allowing us to wrap ourselves in his comfort.

5. **Acceptance** – "I see that my life won't ever be the same, but maybe good will come from this." Acceptance is not resignation or giving up. It is a time of understanding and relaxing with the change. It says yes to the life God has given you.

Read through these steps several times, and consider which of them might describe you. Pray about them, sharing your emotions with God and asking him to do his work in you. You might also talk about them with a good friend or family member.

If you identify with one of these steps, you are not alone. Christian brothers and sisters stand ready to walk with you. Even more importantly, Jesus Christ has experienced it all before you. Victory is yours in him! "Thanks be to God, who gives us the victory through our Lord Jesus Christ" (1 Corinthians 15:57).

Lesson

2

JESUS IDENTIFIES WITH OUR SORROW

We are to God the fragrance of Christ.
The world can't see Jesus endure suffering with grace
because he's not here on earth, but you and I are.

—JONI EARECKSON TADA[1]

TAKEAWAY:
God wants to bring good from our suffering
as we lean into him and trust him with the results.

In this lesson, we see Jesus as our fellow-sufferer who identifies with all our struggles. Isaiah 53:3 says, "He was despised and rejected by men; a man of sorrows, and acquainted with grief." It is natural to wonder why God allowed his Son to endure such affliction and pain. But Jesus suffered willingly on the cross to become "the source of eternal salvation to all who obey him" (Hebrews 5:9). So in your loneliest, darkest hour, you can rest assured that Jesus understands, cares, and has a plan of redemption.

✳ ✳ ✳ ✳

Now read the article below on your own, completing the exercise at the end (NOTE: You may want to divide up responsibility for different parts of the exercise and then share your answers). Also reflect on the questions or write down some brief answers. When the group is ready, share some of your thoughts if you're comfortable doing so.

"Be sober-minded; be watchful.
Your adversary the devil prowls around like a roaring lion,
seeking someone to devour" (1 Peter 5:8).

When Life Isn't Fair

Think back to your teenage years. What is your favorite memory? For many people, it is a favorite family vacation or a summer camp with friends. These weeklong events are planned, anticipated, captured in photos, and retold through the years as great adventures. This is how it should have gone for forty of the teenagers who attended youth camp in 1987 on the Guadalupe River in Texas. But sadly, their week of worship and fun quickly became their worst nightmare when a flash flood swallowed up their van. Ten teenagers lost their lives that morning, making it one of the deadliest natural disasters to hit the Texas Hill Country.

Chip Asberry, then age fifteen, recalls the last night of camp. The pastor said he felt led to press the teens to get right with God—for some, it was their last chance. As the flood hit, Asberry crawled out of the van, struggling to keep his head above water. He saw the rapid current take one friend under and then another. Eventually, he grabbed a branch and pulled himself forty feet up into a tree. From his perch, he prayed, "God, just let me out of this and I'll do whatever you want me to do, no matter what it is."[2]

You may be thinking: Wait a minute! These were Christian kids who earned money to go to camp. They spent the week in Bible study and worship, singing about the love of Jesus. Then, ten kids drowned! That seems so unfair!

For weeks after the flood, Asberry and his friends attended more funerals than any teenager should have to endure. Eventually, the new school year brought a sense of normalcy, but it would take years for these young survivors to recover their faith. Some never did.

SATAN'S WAR WITH THE KINGDOM OF GOD

With every generation, Hollywood movies seem to introduce a new cast of scary villains. From Dracula to Freddy Krueger, to Heath Ledger's eerie portrayal of the Joker, or even scary clowns, people get caught up in fantasizing about evil. Such films encourage us to tuck all things satanic in a box marked "fiction." According to the Barna Group, the majority of American Christians do not believe Satan is a real being.[3]

But it is evident in the Old and New Testaments that Satan is real, and he is always at war with the kingdom of God. His battle plan is to destroy humankind. His demonic forces harass and torment people, tempting them to do all kinds of evil. Second Corinthians 4:4 describes Satan as the god of this world who blinds people from seeing the gospel Jesus came to bring us. And although Jesus was the beloved Son of God who lived a sinless life, he did not escape this satanic war.

Let's consider the different kinds of suffering Jesus experienced, which we discussed in lesson 1: physical, spiritual, emotional, and social.

Read the following descriptions and Bible passages, and IDENTIFY the kind of suffering Jesus endured in each:

P = physical, SP = spiritual, E = emotional, or SO = social.

Example: __SO__ Jesus lived as a refugee in Egypt (see Matthew 2:13–15).

If you want, assign some group members to look up some passages while others look up other passages, and then share your results. For some passages, more than one category may apply, such as in John 8:57–59 where Jesus was in physical danger as a social outcast.

1. __E__ Jesus knew that his coming had caused the death of many baby boys in and around Bethlehem (Matthew 2:16–18).
2. __Sr/P__ Jesus was tempted by Satan after forty days of fasting (Matthew 4:1–11).
3. __SO__ People believed that Jesus was a deceiver, and plotted against him (John 11:45–53; Matthew 12:14).
4. __SO__ The people of his hometown rejected him (Mark 6:1–6).
5. __P|E__ People tried to stone him (John 8:57–59; 10:31–39).
6. __E__ Jesus's heart ached over Jerusalem's terrible future (Matthew 23:37–39).
7. __So|E|Sp__ Jesus was overwhelmed with sorrow and loneliness in Gethsemane (Matthew 26:38–40).
8. __So|E__ Jesus was abandoned by his disciples when the crowd came to him in Gethsemane (Matthew 26:47–56).
9. __So|Sr__ False witnesses accused him during his trial (Matthew 26:60).
10. __P__ Despite his innocence, Jesus was spat on, struck with fists, slapped, beaten, and mocked (Matthew 26:67–68; 27:30–31).
11. __P|So|SrE__ Roman soldiers crucified Jesus (Matthew 27:32–35).
12. __SO__ Jesus was separated from his Father because of the sin of the world that he bore for our sake (Matthew 27:45–46).

REFLECTION QUESTIONS:

How did Jesus respond to those who hurt him?

- Father, forgive them.
- Grace

How have your personal experiences with suffering been similar to those of Jesus?

- Fear
- Hurt

After sharing some responses, have someone read aloud as you complete the rest of the lesson together, or take turns reading.

Lesson

BIBLE FOUNDATION

Jesus Understands Suffering

In our darkest hour, when human comfort fails to touch the depth of our pain, Jesus stands with open arms as the ultimate expression of empathy. Hebrews 4:15 says, "For we do not have a high priest who is unable to sympathize with our weaknesses, but one who in every respect has been tempted as we are, yet without sin." While on earth, the sinless Son of God suffered all the consequences of sin in infinite measure to identify with our anguish, misery, and pain.

Have you ever felt you've disappointed God too many times? While on earth, Jesus lived as a human being, so he completely understands our frailty and mistakes. The writer of Hebrews assures us that Jesus was like us in every respect, and "because he himself has suffered when tempted, he is able to help those who are being tempted" (Hebrews 2:18).

DISCUSSION QUESTION:

Have someone read Hebrews 2:14–18 aloud. According to this passage, what has Jesus accomplished for us through his suffering?

God planned to redeem the world through Christ's suffering. Let's identify some of the benefits of suffering in our lives.

- **Our suffering reveals the life of Christ.** Others can see Jesus in us. God builds strength, virtue, compassion, faith, and sacrificial love in us so we can lift up Jesus in a hurting world.
- **Suffering leads others to Christ.** We can fill up in our flesh what is lacking in his afflictions (Colossians 1:24), and in so doing become that sweet fragrance with the aroma of Christ to God. What a blessing, a privilege, an honor!
- **Suffering cultivates brokenness and dependence on God.** Brokenness is a prerequisite for a follower of Christ. The cross is a symbol of suffering (Luke 9:23), which deepens our faith.
- **Suffering transforms us into Christ's likeness.** Our highest calling is to be transformed into the image of Christ, which occurs through sharing in his suffering (Philippians 3:10).
- **Suffering teaches us compassion for others.** When we trust God with our struggles, we reveal him as a God of supreme worth who is important enough to love and obey despite the hardships. As Christ humbled himself, we identify with him and carry his scars (Philippians 2:5–8).
- **Suffering gives us an eternal perspective.** We can't love God with all our hearts and love the world too. It was this eternal perspective that allowed Christ to humble himself through suffering, even to the point of death (2 Corinthians 4:16–18).

THE
WITNESS

Praying Through Suffering

Captain Ryan Voltin is a tall, powerful-looking Marine Corps attack helicopter pilot—a man of quiet courage with a desire to protect and defend. But one look at him and you know he has paid a heavy price to serve his country.

While serving in Iraq, Captain Voltin deployed to Jordan. On May 25, 2007, he was severely wounded during training exercises when his Cobra helicopter was mistakenly targeted and shot down by friendly fire. Seconds after the bomb hit, flames engulfed the plane. The captain remembers immediately praying that death would come quickly before everything went silent. He suffered third-degree burns to his arms, head, and face. His left leg had to be amputated below the knee. He was hospitalized for two years and has undergone more than twenty surgeries.

Like Jesus in the Garden of Gethsemane, Captain Voltin felt over-whelmed with agony and questioned God's plan for him. "Your prayers may not be answered as you thought or wanted them to be," Voltin says, "but having faith that God's will is being done opened my eyes to more of God's presence. I learned to trust in his will in his time."

Never do we pray more earnestly than when we're in the crucible of affliction and pain. Watch how Captain Voltin and his family experienced the sustaining power of prayer in the most difficult and frightening situation (Video Two at joniandfriends.org/gospel-hard-times).

Captain Voltin and his wife, Pam, are living a devastating reality with countless treatments, therapies, and surgeries. Progress comes in small victories. However, they have seen prayer move the heart of God to change things—even to change people. As Pam looks at her husband with all his injuries, she says, "We are in it to win it."

DISCUSSION QUESTIONS:

- Have you experienced your own Gethsemane? Where and when?
- On the darkest day of your life, how did God reveal his will in his time?

REDEMPTION IN THE FACE OF SUFFERING

Most of the teenagers rescued from the flood waters in Comfort, Texas, spent years struggling with post-traumatic stress disorder, survivor's guilt, and doubts about God. One young woman admitted that she spent a decade living in fear for her and her children's safety before she found peace. Others completely lost faith in God and walked away from the church. One young man confessed that he continues to believe in God in theory, but not in practice. Chip Asberry could have gone that route, but his faith held through the storm.

Like the others, Asberry initially questioned why God would allow such a terrible thing to happen. He stayed connected with his church, continuing to volunteer in the children's ministry. He attended a Bible college for a year and eventually went to work for a company that restores homes after fires or water damage. "We have a tendency to meet people on the worst day of their lives," Asberry said. "It's definitely a calling and a ministry. I do think that God is the best at making lemonade out of lemons, and making as much good come out of tragedy as possible."[4]

When faced with the ultimate sacrifice, Jesus struggled in prayer at Gethsemane, telling his disciples that his soul was crushed with grief to the point of death. In his humanity, he too asked the *why* questions. Why me? Why now? Why this? In the end, he surrendered to the will and purposes of God, saying "Abba, Father, all things are possible for you. Remove this cup from me. Yet not what I will, but what you will" (Mark 14:36). The human agony Jesus endured, as well as his utter surrender to God even unto death, is our roadmap through every affliction we have suffered or will suffer.

Lesson

PRAYER FOCUS

Pray about some of the items below as you close your time together, or include them in your prayers during the coming week.

- Thank God for the Lamb that was slain. Praise God for Christ's sufferings and all that his scars purchased for you, including eternal life (John 1:29).
- Pray for those whose affliction and pain have driven them away from God. Ask God to open their blind eyes to see the light of the gospel (2 Corinthians 4:4).
- Ask Jesus to help you forgive anyone who has hurt you, knowing they deserve the same kind of mercy that he extends to you (Matthew 6:12).
- Pray for America's disabled veterans and their families. Thank God for the freedoms we enjoy, especially our freedom to worship as we please (1 Timothy 2:1–2).

The action plan below includes a writing exercise that can help you connect with this lesson between now and the next meeting, when you will have a chance to share about it if you wish to do so.

Hidden Sorrows of the Heart

Jesus related to the brokenness of the Samaritan woman, the grief of Mary and Martha, the betrayal of Judas, the denial of Peter, and the doubts of Thomas (John 4, 11, 18, 20). He sees and understands the unspoken sorrow in your heart, too.

Many Christians find it helpful to write about their inner pain in a prayer or a letter to Jesus. Thank him for understanding your innermost heart and ask him to guide you through the situation. Whether you destroy your writings or share them with a trusted friend, the act of writing to Jesus affirms your faith and builds your trust in him who knows everything about you.

David Lyons lost his twelve-year-old son Ian to cancer in 2009, and two years later his sister Linda also died of cancer. He describes how it feels to pray through extraordinary pain:

> Praying in the face of pain leads us into new spiritual territory, where we learn to pray under fire, to pray for miracles, to pray when we're worn out, to pray through our motives, to pray through our anxieties. Much of what happens through our prayer happens in us. God uses prayer to change us.

The image in my mind is that of a little girl sitting in the midst of a raging battle. Bombs explode and bullets whiz by, but she does not move. She's waiting. She's waiting for her dad, who she knows will keep her safe. And we wait. We wait knowing that nothing will keep our Daddy from accomplishing what he intends. We know he will keep us safe. We're taking him at his word.[5]

Praise God he knows where you are sitting today and what it is you wait for. Trust him with childlike faith.

Wait for the LORD; be strong,
and let your heart take courage;
wait for the LORD! (Psalm 27:14)

3

AN EVER-PRESENT HELP

*Admittedly, the Lord doesn't always solve
our problems instantaneously, and he sometimes permits
us to walk through the valley of the shadow of death.
But he is there with us even in the darkest hours,
and we can never escape his encompassing love.*

—DR. JAMES DOBSON[1]

TAKEAWAY:

With God forever by your side, you can face any difficulty.

In this lesson, we'll consider how our Good Shepherd knows the way through life's valleys. While we tend to give in to sadness and isolation, the Good Shepherd is always beside us, prodding us to higher ground. He never forgets or abandons his own. He knows his sheep and leads each one to new strengths in difficult seasons. As we follow Jesus, we remember his gentle faithfulness and give thanks in every circumstance.

* * * *

Read the article below on your own until you get to the reflection questions. Think about your answers, or write them down. Be prepared to share some of your thoughts with the group when everyone is ready.

Anne Graham Lotz was diagnosed with breast cancer in 2018. Faced with the unknowns ahead, a hymn she'd copied into her first Bible as a child brought Anne comfort.

> Trust Him when dark doubts assail thee.
> Trust Him when thy strength is small.
> Trust Him when to simply trust Him
> Is the hardest thing of all.
>
> Trust Him, He is ever faithful.
> Trust Him for His will is best.
> Trust Him for the heart of Jesus
> Is the only place to rest.
>
> Trust Him then through tears and sunshine,
> All thy cares upon Him cast,
> 'Til the storms of life are over,
> And the trusting days are past.

"As I follow the Good Shepherd through this Valley of the Shadow, I am firmly fixing my eyes on Jesus with a heart of absolute trust."[2]

**HARD TIMES
IN THE
WORLD**

The Promises
of the Shepherd

If "the LORD is my shepherd; I shall not want" (Psalm 23:1), why am I going through this? Where is Jesus when I need him?

Lynda Ryan, a playwright and producer, directed annual passion plays for many years in Orlando, Florida. Her powerful dramas have inspired audiences as they witnessed Jesus's journey to Calvary and felt the presence of God. In the final scene, as Jesus ascends into heaven saying, "Behold, I am with you always" (Matthew 28:20), a media presentation depicts Jesus (the actor) alongside hurting people in real time. Jesus stands with a family in front of a pile of ash that was once their beautiful home. Jesus puts his hand on the shoulder of an army private before he is deployed to a war-torn country. Jesus pushes the wheelchair of a pale, thin preschooler in the hall of a cancer hospital. Jesus helps a businessman pack up items from his desk after losing his job.

Where do you need to picture Jesus with you today?

Jesus never lost his job or watched his home burn. He never had cancer or served in the military. But he is intimately involved with our heartaches. If we quiet our hearts in the midst of disappointment and sorrow, we too can hear him whisper, "I am with you always."

LOST SHEEP NEED A SHEPHERD

The world's skeptics say trusting God is a crutch for the weak: Bible stories about Jesus are fiction, designed for the poor, the mournful, and the meek. This thinking is reinforced by the idea that people can't possibly understand God, let alone follow some secret plan for their lives.

It's true—hard times can harden people. One minute, life is good; the next, life slams us into a brick wall. God doesn't pretend that life is a picnic with green grass and butterflies. He said we would walk through valleys with dark shadows. In hard times, we can quickly become lost like defenseless sheep without a shepherd.

The experiences of Neil and Bethany are not uncommon in today's world. While both were raised in Christian families, they lost their way and desperately needed the Good Shepherd's comfort.

Neil, a fourteen-year-old whose dreams of being a quarterback were crushed, says: "My life got turned upside down when a deranged neighbor got mad at my dad and shot at our house. A bullet hit my spine leaving me paralyzed from my chest down. I used to go to church, but no more. God doesn't listen to me. The only way I can numb my pain is with alcohol, marijuana, and crystal meth."

Bethany was already struggling in middle school when her parents decided to divorce. With all of the turmoil they were experiencing in their own lives, her parents didn't notice that Bethany had started cutting herself. When a concerned friend tried to assure Bethany that God was still there for her, she lashed out: "Why should I believe God cares about me when my own parents don't even care?"

According to a study done by the Centers for Disease Control and Prevention, the suicide rate for ten-to-seventeen-year-olds increased 70 percent from 2006 to 2016. Experts attribute the rise to societal issues such as insufficient mental health screening, polarizing environments, poverty, and drug addiction by parents and teens.[3]

Statistics like these must sadden God's heart. He created families to live in harmony and protect one another. He did not send his Son into the world to judge us, but to give us eternal life (see John 3:16–17).

Jesus described God as a shepherd who cares about his lost sheep: "What man of you, having a hundred sheep, if he has lost one of them, does not leave the ninety-nine in the open country, and go after the one that is lost, until he finds it? And when he has found it, he lays it on his shoulders, rejoicing" (Luke 15:4–5).

The shepherd in that parable searched for one lost sheep until he found him. Joni Eareckson Tada has experienced the tenacity of Jesus that always works for our good. She shares her insight: "The Good Shepherd never lets us down. He never betrays us nor torments us. Never ever is he out to harm you. He seeks only your good. He removed the only kind of suffering that can ever really harm us: and that is, separation from him. This means that now, all suffering comes only to make our souls great; and teach us how to learn to bend to his will."

REFLECTION QUESTIONS:

Are you feeling lost, suffering alone in a difficult season?

What do you need to trust in Jesus regardless of the circumstances?

Can you believe he is searching for you, waiting to rejoice over you?

If you want to, share some of your responses with the group. Then have someone read aloud, or take turns reading, to complete the rest of the lesson together.

BIBLE FOUNDATION

3

The Goodness of the Shepherd

When Jesus said, "I am the Good Shepherd," he set himself apart from all other shepherds: "The thief comes only to steal and kill and destroy. I came that they may have life and have it abundantly. I am the good shepherd. The good shepherd lays down his life for the sheep. He who is a hired hand and not a shepherd, who does not own the sheep, sees the wolf coming and leaves the sheep and flees, and the wolf snatches them and scatters them. He flees because he is a hired hand and cares nothing for the sheep. I am the good shepherd. I know my own and my own know me" (John 10:10–14).

In ancient times, many shepherds were hired hands, not sheep owners. Their job was to protect and defend the sheep, which are by nature defenseless and dependent on the shepherd. As a young shepherd, David killed lions and bears to protect the sheep (see 1 Samuel 17:36). Unlike hired hands, who often ran from danger, David willingly put his life at risk for the sheep. But David can't compare to Jesus, the Good Shepherd whose goodness is unique—noble, wholesome, and righteous.

While it appeared that the thief had stolen Neil and Bethany from the sheepfold, their Good Shepherd never abandoned them. The prayers of their family and friends surrounded them until they safely returned to Jesus Christ.

Eventually, Neil trusted Jesus as his Savior and sought help for his addictions. He later felt called to ministry and attended Biola University in California where he studied organizational leadership with a specialization in addiction studies among people with disabilities. While at Biola, Neil served as an intern with our Joni and Friends Cause 4 Life program.[4]

After a friend from church informed their youth pastor about her cutting, Bethany's parents found a therapist to help her learn to process her emotions. Now, as a college student, Bethany writes a blog that helps other teens keep from spiraling into depression and turning to self-mutilation.

Did you notice how God not only restored Neil and Bethany to the faith but also called them to places of service? Jesus did the same with the disciple Peter, who had denied Jesus three times:

> When they had finished breakfast, Jesus said to Simon Peter, "Simon, son of John, do you love me more than these?" He said to him, "Yes, Lord; you know that I love you." He said to him, "Feed my lambs." He said to him a second time, "Simon, son of John, do you love me?" He said to him, "Yes, Lord; you know that I love you." He said to him, "Tend my sheep." He said to him the third time, "Simon, son of John, do you love me?" Peter was grieved because he said to him the third time, "Do you love me?" and he said to him, "Lord, you know everything; you know that I love you." Jesus said to him, "Feed my sheep." (John 21:15–17)

Peter must have been taken aback by Jesus's question. Jesus had welcomed him back and reinstated him in the eyes of the other disciples. Was he now questioning Peter's love? No, Jesus was calling Peter to his mission in life. Peter was to love those Jesus loved—his sheep. Lambs can't feed themselves; they need a shepherd. In the same way, Jesus was saying new believers don't know how to feed on God's truth; they need a shepherd to teach them.

DISCUSSION QUESTIONS:

- Is there an area where Jesus is calling you to get out of your comfort zone and become a shepherd?
- Do you know of some new believers in need of a mentor, a teacher, a friend?

THE WITNESS

A Call to Feed God's Sheep

Mary Jane Ponten was born with cerebral palsy at a time when the knowledge base for her condition was virtually nonexistent. Her story is one of persistence and a demonstration of what life can become through faith in Christ. Mary Jane accepted her limitations, but with the help of a supportive family, she also determined to become all God had planned for her. As a child, she dreamed of becoming a missionary to China. But when she eventually applied to mission agencies, none of them would accept her because of her disability. Sixty years later, God used Mary Jane's disability to help her connect with Joni and Friends and serve as a missionary in China. Now in her eighties, she continues to minister throughout the world as God calls her to serve.

Watch a video that highlights Mary Jane's resolve as she refused to give up on the dreams God had given her (Video Three at joniand-friends.org/gospel-hard-times). Then discuss the questions below.

DISCUSSION QUESTIONS:

- How has Mary Jane Ponten been able to feed God's sheep?

• Did she challenge any preconceived notions you might have about people affected by disability?

My God will supply every need of yours according to his riches in glory in Christ Jesus. (Philippians 4:19)

PRAYER FOCUS

As part of your closing prayer time, you might pray David's prayer in Psalm 119:175–176.

> Let my soul live and praise you,
>   and let your rules help me.
> I have gone astray like a lost sheep; seek your servant,
>   for I do not forget your commandments.

You also might write down a few sentences about times the Good Shepherd provided for you. Meditate on the goodness of God and give thanks.

Completing some of the suggestions in the action plan below will help you stay involved with what you have learned, on your own, until the next time the group meets. You will have a chance to share about it at that time.

Lesson

ACTION
PLAN

Seeking the Shepherd

- Practice the presence of God. This may mean turning off all media and digital devices in favor of the discipline of silence. The world calls this *mindfulness* and people take classes to learn to be "in the moment." This idea is not new. Meditation did not begin with yoga; it's an ancient biblical tradition. Psalm 19:14 says, "Let the words of my mouth and the meditation of my heart be acceptable in your sight, O LORD, my rock and my redeemer."

- Play worship songs that remind you of the presence of God. Joni Eareckson Tada is especially fond of the old hymns because their messages are so rich in Scriptures. Joni has compiled a list of her favorites, including the lyrics, on her blog at www. joniandfriends.org/jonis-corner/jonis-favorite-hymns/.

- Discover how to reach out, bring in people who are struggling, and point them to Jesus as their ever-present help in suffering. It may be regularly sending encouragement cards to an exhausted, young mother. It could be a bi-monthly lunch appointment with a man searching for a job to support his family. It could be taking a tall mocha latte to an elderly woman who has no family and can no longer drive. Remember to include Scriptures that have inspired you to walk with the Lord.

4

A PLACE OF HEALING

*If God tears up your game plan and leads you
into a valley instead of onto a mountaintop,
it is because he wants you to discover his plan, which
is more beautiful than anything
you could have dreamed up.*

—BRENNAN MANNING[1]

TAKEAWAY:
When we experience comfort and healing,
God calls us to comfort others.

In this lesson, we examine God's call to lay down our heavy burdens
and remove the masks that prevent us from living authentic lives.
Whether we face chronic pain, mental disorders, broken relationships, or isolation due to a disability, suffering can prevent us from
fully participating in life, as well as in the family of God. Only as we
embrace the biblical meaning of healing can we comfort others and
transform our churches into places of healing and hope.

* * * *

Read the article below on your own, and consider the reflection questions or write down some answers. Be ready to share some of your thoughts when the group is ready.

Living on the Edge

Ellen's knuckles were white as she whipped the steering wheel of her Lexus into the hospital parking lot. Grabbing her purse, she ran toward the bright red *emergency* sign. Recognizing Ellen, the nurse led her through the double doors to a small room where her husband, Brian, lay pale and motionless. The attending physician signed papers, transferring Brian to the critical care unit. Then, gently taking Ellen's hand, the doctor said, "This is the third time Brian has tried to take his own life, and this time he may succeed. We've done all we can for now."

Through the long night, Ellen's emotions seesawed between utter panic and seething anger. She'd loved Brian since the day they were married nineteen years earlier. He was caring, kind, and smart—a wonderful father and a successful businessman. As founder and CEO of a multimillion-dollar corporation, he managed a worldwide sales team. They both struggled to figure out why Brian had changed from a confident leader at the top of his game to a listless, fearful shell of his former self. Even with the parade of doctors, tests, medications, and counselors, his depression and withdrawal had intensified.

Ellen knew her anger stemmed from her fear of losing him and how their teenage son and daughter would cope. Sitting outside Brian's room day after day, Ellen replayed the last few weeks in her mind.

Even if Brian wanted to give up, she couldn't let him. Wouldn't let him. *I have to do something, but what?* In that moment, she had a strange flashback to her grandmother, who died when Ellen was ten. On visits to Grandma's house, they had always gone to church and read Bible stories at bedtime. Although she hadn't been to church since, it was a sweet memory—one that brought Ellen off her chair in search of a Bible. The hospital chaplain was happy to give her one. So as Brian slowly regained his strength, Ellen kept a faithful vigil by his door, reading God's Word every day.

MYTHS ABOUT HEALING

Jesus said, "Come to me, all who labor and are heavy laden, and I will give you rest. Take my yoke upon you, and learn from me, for I am gentle and lowly in heart, and you will find rest for your souls. For my yoke is easy and my burden is light" (Matthew 11:28–30).

But in suffering's darkest hour, those words can seem like a joke. Suffering is not easy or light, and dying can be labored and heavy laden. So what is Jesus trying to say? And when the Bible promises that God will deliver us from trouble, what does that look like?

First, Jesus is saying, "Come to me and find rest." It's okay to seek all forms of qualified medical help, but don't run here and there reaching for every advice you read on the internet or hear from friends. Put Jesus at the top of the list of helpers. Second, consider the value of sharing your burden with a close friend who has experienced everything you are going through. Jesus Christ is that friend.

Those of us raised in church may have preconceived ideas about divine healing that can be misleading and even detrimental. One of the most harmful myths about physical healing is the notion that if people have enough faith, they will be healed. This view reasons that sickness is the work of Satan and Jesus came to destroy the works of evil. Jesus healed people during his time on earth, and God never changes. Therefore, we have the promise that whatever we ask in Jesus name will be done. So, if we ask and are not healed, we may conclude there's something wrong with us. These ideas are preached in many churches, causing countless Christians to question their faith.

Authenticity is lost when people feel they can't be honest about their ongoing struggles for fear of judgment or condemnation. Often, the greatest rest and deliverance we receive is the spiritual rest of coming to Christ and his church. His eternal comfort outweighs the sufferings of this life, painful as they are.

REFLECTION QUESTIONS:

Think of a time in your life when you felt as distraught and helpless as Ellen and Brian. Did you mask your real feelings from others or God? In what ways?

Did God feel near or distant?

How did the experience change you?

Share some of your thoughts, and then begin working through the rest of the lesson together. Have someone read aloud, or let several people take turns.

BIBLE FOUNDATION

The Church as a Healing Place

Have prayers for your healing (or a loved one's) gone unanswered? Note the questions about physical healing that you've wrestled with.

____ I prayed for healing, but my condition didn't improve. Is there sin in my life?

____ Am I praying the wrong way or using the wrong words?

____ Is there something else I should do to find healing?

____ Are other Christians judging me because I'm still sick and depressed?

This kind of mental anguish can take its toll on us. As Christ's followers, we need to look to one source to understand healing—the Bible. In many recorded stories, Jesus healed men and women suffering from physical and mental conditions. There are even accounts of mass physical healings in the New Testament where Jesus healed many people (Matthew 8:16–17; Mark 1:32–34). He also dismissed the notion that sickness and disabilities must be due to divine punishment, curses, or demonization (John 9:1–5). But Jesus didn't heal everyone who came to him. Moreover, those he did heal eventually died.

God revealed himself as Jehovah Rapha ("The Lord our Healer") and he continues to heal sicknesses and diseases according to his sovereign purpose. Yet, it is a mystery why some receive healing and others do not. Healing is ultimately God's decision. In her book *A Place of Healing*, Joni Eareckson Tada shares what she's discovered:

> The *real* question, of course, is not whether God can heal or does heal; it is whether or not God *wills* to heal all those who truly come to Him in faith. . . .
>
> Let me state my answer to the question—the real question—in just twelve words. . . .
>
> Here is what I believe: *God reserves the right to heal or not . . . as He sees fit.*
>
> There are times when I feel almost sure I know what would be best in a given situation. . . .
>
> But the fact is I only know so much, I only understand so much, I only see so much, and I only grasp so much of what I do see. With [the apostle] Paul I sometimes have to cry out, "Oh, the depth of the riches of the wisdom and knowledge of God! How unsearchable his judgments, and his paths beyond tracing out!" (Romans 11:33 NIV).[2]

God may decide not to heal a person while on earth for reasons we do not always understand. However, a more in-depth look into the Scriptures reveals that true healing is an inward journey that has more to do with the heart and soul than the physical body. Our souls live forever; our earthly bodies do not.

Although physical wellness is encouraged and should be sought, true biblical health and wholeness relate primarily to the spirit. For example, Paul's physical body was broken after years of beatings and poor treatment. He reminded the Corinthians that our bodies are like temporary tents—our new, eternal bodies will be in heaven (see 2 Corinthians 5:1).

Spiritual healing begins with a right relationship with God, which is salvation. It also consists of a right relationship with others, especially those in our faith communities. Jesus prayed for believers "that they may all be one, just as you, Father, are in me, and I in you, that they may also be in us" (John 17:21).

God calls the church to minister to those who are hurting. He has not called us to cure every physical need. Instead, he has called us to bring spiritual healing to one another through prayer, ministering the gospel, and teaching God's Word and ways.

In biblical times, people with disease or disabilities were often excluded from community life. But a large part of a person's spiritual healing involved restoring him or her to community. When a physical cure was the means to accomplish this, then Jesus did so. Otherwise, his ministry was to the heart and soul. The Bible teaches us to pray for the sick and the suffering. Whether God heals a person physically while on earth or chooses to reveal his power through their weakness, this is up to him. He works out everything in conformity with his eternal will.

Second Corinthians 1:3–4 says, "Blessed be the God and Father of our Lord Jesus Christ, the Father of mercies and God of all comfort, who comforts us in all our affliction, so that we may be able to comfort those who are in any affliction, with the comfort with which we ourselves are comforted by God." This tells us that when we've experienced comfort and healing, God calls us to comfort others. Our churches should be places where all people feel safe enough to open their hearts to Jesus and live in unity with the family of God.

Christians don't treat hurting people as the world does. Why? Because we have a God of comfort, who comforts us in our suffering, so we can comfort others—the legacy of faith to the next generation. If you've ever sat by the bedside of a saintly grandparent in their last days, this concept rings true. "Precious in the sight of the LORD is the death of his saints" (Psalm 116:15).

DISCUSSION QUESTION:

What are some ways that coming to Jesus, and being part of his family, give an even greater rest than an immediate end to our current sufferings might give?

Lesson

THE WITNESS

Open Doors, Open Hearts

While serving as senior pastor for the First Church of the Nazarene in Pasadena, California, Dr. Scott Daniels saw the potential impact of believers who are willing to come alongside those enduring difficult seasons or suffering. He came to understand the isolation felt by many families who have children with disabilities. "These families are limited in the places they can go within the community to find connection due to the challenges they face," says Dr. Daniels. "As our church truly becomes a genuine community, we're capable of bringing encouragement and healing."

For a glimpse into the lives of families affected by disability and how the church can be a safe haven during life's storms, watch this lesson's video clip (Video Four at joniandfriends.org/gospel-hard-times). Then discuss the questions below.

DISCUSSION QUESTIONS:

- What could the church have done to help the single mother in the video so that she would feel welcome and encouraged to attend?

- Has there been a time of struggle in your own family when you wished someone at your church would have reached out, or do you have an example of a time when they did?

In a society hyper-focused on controlling our image, we like to look as if we "have it all together," and we certainly don't like to ask for help. For those in positions of authority within a church, or in an esteemed position within their community, it can be even harder to acknowledge weakness and let others come alongside.

Ellen had waited years for Brian to realize his powerlessness. She had witnessed his valiant fight to hide his depression at home and in the office. But when he came home from the hospital, he seemed ready to wave the white flag of surrender. This gave Ellen the courage she needed to share what God was doing in her heart. One afternoon as they drank iced tea on the patio, Ellen told Brian about how she had started reading the Bible outside the door of his hospital room and the peace her daily reading continued to provide.

They started reading God's Word together, and after a few months Brian and Ellen began attending church. At first, they slipped in after the service started and left before it ended. They didn't sign a visitor card or shake anyone's hand.

As Christmas rolled around, they made an appointment to meet with the pastor. Ellen shared their story of hitting rock bottom and finding God's grace and mercy. Brian said, "Pastor, I credit the beautiful music of your choir and orchestra and your down-to-earth sermons with helping save my life. I've got a long way to go, but I'm so grateful. We want to make a Christmas donation to help the church."

The pastor was happy to accept the donation, but more intent on getting Brian and Ellen connected with others in the church. He invited Brian to join their weekly businessmen's breakfast and Bible study, where he was introduced to another man who had battled depression. Dennis, a recovering alcoholic with a sharp wit and a strong list of credentials, was exactly who Brian needed to help him understand God's grace and the path to true healing.

"When we come to the end of ourselves, we come to the beginning of God." —Billy Graham[3]

PRAYER FOCUS

As part of your closing prayer time today, consider writing down the names of three people who need God's comfort and healing. Pray for them.

Ask God how you might be of comfort to someone this week. Watch for his answer and be ready to act.

Between now and the next time the group meets, use the action plan to start putting what you've learned in this lesson into action.

ACTION PLAN

Building Healthy Relationships

While each of us faces unique challenges, we all have one thing in common—our need for genuine relationships. God designed us to live in community. As we remove our emotional masks and share our joys and sorrows with others, friendships deepen and respect grows. We also have more significant opportunities to minister to one another.

- If you are going through a difficult season and feel isolated or alone, begin praying for God to help you be transparent about your struggles with a fellow believer who can walk with you.
- Consider ways you can intentionally reach out to someone going through hard times. Write down one thing you could do to befriend him or her.
- Set aside some time to learn more about your church's compassion ministries and where you could get involved.

Lesson

5

BRING IN THE BROKEN

*If the church is going to fulfill its God-given mission
in our modern world, we are going to have to take
our responsibility to one another seriously. We
will have to accept his call to bear one another's
burdens—even when it's messy, even when
we find ourselves in over our heads.*

—FRANCIS CHAN[1]

┌─────────────────── **TAKEAWAY:** ───────────────────┐

We should seek to bring into our communities
those who are excluded and marginalized.

└──┘

In this lesson, we discover that God's mission for the church includes
all people, especially those who are treated unjustly by society. In
Jesus's time on earth, he often stopped to help the sick, poor, and
disabled. In Luke 14:12–24, he used a parable to give his followers a
powerful mandate about welcoming and including people who are
marginalized and disabled into the life of the church.

Lesson

**HARD TIMES
IN THE
WORLD**

Jesus, Open Our Eyes

In our media-driven society, where Facebook friends parade their "perfect" lives, it is easy to overlook the lonely and broken people around us. We brush shoulders with them every day in grocery stores, schools, workplaces, and gas stations, but have no idea the burdens they carry. Some struggles are obvious, such as people begging on street corners or staggering under the influence of alcohol or drugs. Other hurts are not so easy to spot, such as people suffering from chronic pain, mental illness, or the exhaustion and grief of caregiving. According to the U. S. Census Bureau,

- One in five Americans live with some type of disability.
- More than five million children under age fifteen have a disability; half are classified as severe.
- Four and a half million veterans received disability benefits in 2015.
- Ten million people a year experience a serious mental illness.
- Sixty-five million Americans provide care for someone with a disability or chronic disease.[2]

While these statistics are on the rise, the people they represent rarely come up in our daily conversations. Why? Could it be because we tend to ignore what we fear? We get stuck trying to balance compassion and pity, with a desperate hope that we will never find ourselves in similar circumstances. Children, on the other hand, naturally express their curiosity and concern, asking, "What's wrong with that man?" or, "Why is that lady in a wheelchair?"

It takes courage and compassion to come alongside a person or family while they endure hardships. It is only when we admit our own brokenness that we are able to truly extend God's love to others and see lives transformed. As Christians, we should be asking: Do these hurting people know that Jesus loves them? Have they heard the good news of the gospel? What can we do? What can our churches do?

In our second lesson, we learned that Jesus relates to humanity's suffering because he willingly took the pain of our affliction and sin upon himself at Calvary. Jesus became our role model so we could become his scarred hands and feet in the world. We, the church, are his body—called to love and serve all people in his name.

The core of our call to ministry is the Great Commission in Matthew 28:18–20, to go and make disciples of all nations. But this call goes hand-in-hand with the Luke 14 mandate, which Jesus gave at a meal hosted by religious leaders. There he told the parable of the great banquet, which reflects God's heart for broken people.

> He said also to the man who had invited him, "When you give a dinner or a banquet, do not invite your friends or your brothers or your relatives or rich neighbors, lest they also invite you in return and you be repaid. But when you give a feast, invite the poor, the crippled, the lame, the blind, and you will be blessed, because they cannot repay you. For you will be repaid at the resurrection of the just."
>
> When one of those who reclined at the table with him heard these things, he said to him, "Blessed is everyone who will eat bread in the kingdom of God!" But he said to him, "A man once gave a great banquet and invited many. And at the time for the banquet he sent his servant to say to those

who had been invited, 'Come, for everything is now ready.' But they all alike began to make excuses. The first said to him, 'I have bought a field, and I must go out and see it. Please have me excused.' And another said, 'I have bought five yoke of oxen, and I go to examine them. Please have me excused.' And another said, 'I have married a wife, and therefore I cannot come.' So the servant came and reported these things to his master. Then the master of the house became angry and said to his servant, 'Go out quickly to the streets and lanes of the city, and bring in the poor and crippled and blind and lame.' And the servant said, 'Sir, what you commanded has been done, and still there is room.' And the master said to the servant, 'Go out to the highways and hedges and compel people to come in, that my house may be filled.'" (Luke 14:16–23)

GIVE US EARS TO HEAR

Historically, though, the church has been slow to embrace people with disabilities. European and American societies once viewed them as abnormal, even offensive. They were objects of dread and ridicule, sub-human and diseased, believed to be evil or possessed. The methods used for mass exterminations in the Nazi death camps originated with experimentation on people with physical, emotional, and intellectual disabilities, and with sterilization designed to eliminate such "defects."

Decades of discoveries in education, medicine, and science have initiated significant reforms in how those with disabilities participate in society. Or have they? Even with the 1990 signing of the Americans with Disabilities Act (ADA), progress has been slow and many families continue to face overwhelming obstacles.

While most religions have sacred writings that speak of love, mercy, and benevolent service, many fail to apply these virtues to people with intellectual and physical disorders. Eastern religious teachings are in sharp contrast with biblical teachings. For example, some false teachings view people with disabilities as:

- Having bad karma, needing to be demoted to the lower class.
- Objects of charity to be pitied, a disgrace to the family.
- Non-contributors to society, economically draining and no use to others.
- Cursed and ignored as victims.

Even some Christians see people with afflictions as problems to fix or burdens to endure rather than as people created in the image of God and embraced by Jesus. These friends are our brothers and sisters in Christ, gifted for service; without them the church is incomplete.

Take another look at Luke 14:12–23. Jesus says we are to stop striving to have a "who's who" on our guest lists, and seek to bring into our faith communities those who are marginalized within society—not as a one-time act of compassion, but as a Christ-centered lifestyle. With that passage in mind, reflect on the questions below.

REFLECTION QUESTIONS:

What did the Jewish leaders at the table expect the coming kingdom to reflect?

What were Jesus's expectations of the coming kingdom?

Share some of your responses, and then complete the rest of the lesson together. Have someone read aloud.

Examine Our Hearts

Jesus's teachings in Luke 14 were radical and revolutionary for his day, but they also challenge today's Christians. We must examine our hearts for signs of apathy. With God's help, we can avoid being part of the problem and commit to understanding people whose needs are different from our own—beginning in the church.

Koinonia is a New Testament Greek word which means "communion" or "fellowship" among Christian believers. Paul's letters to the churches admonished believers to build one another up and commune with one another and with God. The church was never meant to be a *place* people merely visit for worship, but rather a shared *community* where friends know one another's joys and burdens (see 1 Thessalonians 5:12–14).

Why are so many churches missing the mark in compassion ministries?

It is not uncommon for church leaders and members to express concerns about opening their doors to people with disabilities and the marginalized. Here are some typical comments:

- Our church does not have the resources or volunteers for these ministries.
- Are these ministries part of our church's core values and vision?

- Volunteers need special education and training in these ministries.
- Other churches in the community already offer programs for special needs and counseling.
- These people will be a burden and can't contribute to our church.

The truth is that congregations are full of people whose gifts and talents are divinely designed to meet every need within the church family. God's love and mercy qualify Christians to reach into their neighborhoods. If we do not take a risk, we do not love people, and we will miss the blessings God promises. Joni Eareckson Tada writes, "Ministry is messy. God plops people with disabilities in the midst of a congregation—a hand grenade that blows apart the picture-perfectness of the church. But these disenfranchised folks are the indispensable part of the body."

In his book, *Dangerous Wonder*, Mike Yaconelli paints a challenging picture of the grace our churches will need in order to include people enduring hard times: "The grace of God is dangerous. It's lavish, excessive, outrageous, and scandalous. God's grace is ridiculously inclusive. Apparently, God doesn't care who he loves. He is not very careful about the people he calls his friends or the people he calls his church."[3]

Isn't that incredible! God's grace covers our brokenness, regardless of our issues. If God does not hold back, how can we withhold his truth from others in need?

DISCUSSION QUESTIONS:

Read each Bible passage. How might you complete each statement to apply that passage in your life? As a group, come up with several good responses for each item.

The LORD is near to the brokenhearted and saves the crushed in spirit. (Psalm 34:18)	When people feel crushed, I can be kind to them, like Jesus, by _having ment & listening 1st_
Restore to me the joy of your salvation, and uphold me with a willing spirit. Then I will teach transgressors your ways, and sinners will return to you. (Psalm 51:12–13)	I can pass the joy and encouragement God has given me along to others by _caring to_ .X
"When you give a feast, invite the poor, the crippled, the lame, the blind, and you will be blessed, because they cannot repay you. For you will be repaid at the resurrection of the just." (Luke 14:13–14)	A practical way I can spend time with the less fortunate, sharing with them and being blessed myself, is _E,R & AGAPE._
"Go out to the highways and hedges and compel people to come in, that my house may be filled." (Luke 14:23)	I can invite outcasts into the fellowship of God's people by _connecting outside the Church_
All have sinned and fall short of the glory of God. (Romans 3:23)	When I'm with needy or hurting people, I can be on level ground with them—a fellow sinner who needs God—by _sharing_ . _my shortcomings —CR._

THE WITNESS

Friendship Evangelism

For people coping with addiction, disease, disability, or grief, going to church can be one of the best or worst experiences of their whole week. Unfortunately, many vulnerable people don't feel welcome at church.

Mark and David both have intellectual disabilities. They came to know and love Jesus at the Light & Power Company Bible class at their church. Jeff and Kathi McNair founded this ministry twenty years ago for adults with disabilities. The group meets regularly to study the Word, talk to God in prayer, and hang out together during the week.

Dr. McNair says, "Teaching adults with intellectual disabilities about Jesus is a privilege, not only because they are generally appreciative, affirming, and enthusiastic, but because of their potential. Since spiritual truths are spiritually—not intellectually—discerned, these students have the same potential for spiritual growth as other church members. Spiritual maturity may look different . . . but it is just as real."[4]

See how Dr. McNair cultivates real friendships that go beyond church walls. Watch Video Five at joniandfriends.org/gospel-hard-times. Then discuss the questions below.

DISCUSSION QUESTIONS:

- What did Mark admit was his biggest fear?
- Do you have friends or coworkers with disabilities? If so, what are some ways you might share your faith and/or just "hang out"?

Before Tom and Blanca Siebels's son James was born, they would have said their church extended God's radical grace to everyone without judgment. Then James was diagnosed with autism, and it became increasingly difficult to maintain a "normal" life. His condition sometimes required two or three therapy sessions a day. Activities such as going out to dinner after church on Sunday became impossible due to James's behavior problems.

Church friends had always been an important part of their lives, so these parents determined to take turns volunteering in James's class. Some Sundays went well, but others were very challenging for James and his teachers. One day James bit a classmate before anyone could stop him. That week a church leader called the Siebels and asked them to stop bringing James to class because ten families had vowed to stop coming if James was there. Tom and Blanca were devastated. Blanca, a relatively new Christian, was so discouraged she wanted to leave the church. However, Tom was not ready to give up on their home church or their son.

Tom and Blanca decided to trust God when times were tough and to keep praying for their church. They held on to hope that some good might result for their family and others. When the disability ministry started, the Siebels said people started to come alongside them and embrace their son. The new special needs director assured these parents that the staff was eager to learn more about James. Eventually, Tom and Blanca were able to enjoy the worship service together without worry. A new support group was started where parents shared about their everyday joys and experiences, as well as the struggles. This special ministry not only changed the lives of the families it served—it changed the church.

One pastor described the disability ministry at his church this way: "At first, I thought we didn't have the resources to reach out in an intentional way to persons and families with special needs. Now, I can't imagine having a church without a ministry to them. Our church has significantly grown in Christ-likeness and numbers as a direct result of the disability ministry."

God wants us to understand the brokenness we all share and our deep need for interdependence on him and one another. No one makes it alone. People dealing with adversity have much to contribute to the body of Christ. Through their lives, God shows his church how to become a mature body. We'll learn more about this in the next lesson.

A friend loves at all times, and a brother is born for adversity. (Proverbs 17:17)

PRAYER FOCUS

Today you might pray that God would help you do the things you came up with in the exercise based on the five Bible passages. You could also pray for others in the following ways:

- Pray for people who have been scarred by false religious teachings or bad church experiences.
- Pray for the millions of caregivers in America supporting people who are unable to care for themselves.
- Pray that more young people will accept God's call to care ministries and be willing to share God's love with those in need.

As you leave, consider some of the ideas and steps given in the action plan below. It is a way for you to put to work what you have learned.

Lesson

**ACTION
PLAN**

5

Meeting the Needs

If your church has compassion ministries, pray about how you might get involved. These ministries may include addiction recovery, parent support, hospital visitation, care for the homeless, grief support, and lay counseling.

If your church does not have a disability ministry, ask friends to join you in prayer for God's help. Awareness begins in the heart. Then, consider these simple steps:

1. Start with a need. Are there people in your church who need special support? Who are those in your community that need help?

2. Choose a model. Decide what kind of ministry model could work best in your church: respite care (a parents' night out), special buddies (one-on-one helpers), parent support group, or a sibling program.

3. Decide what programs might make a good start. For example, if you have children or adults with developmental disabilities, you might begin by adapting Bible studies and social events to meet their needs.

4. Design a Luke 14 banquet for your church or small group. Recruit volunteers to prepare food and decorate tables. Create

table centerpieces and small gift baskets. Invite a set number of people with disabilities and their families. After dinner, give door prizes or gift certificates. Hold a short program highlighting someone's testimony.

NOTE: The Luke 14 mandate makes it clear that people with disabilities are central in the kingdom of God. A church must function as a living and moving organism with the ability to love, forgive, encourage, and support. At the same time, a church is an organization in which divine work is accomplished. When these function in unity, the church can work with God to alleviate suffering (2 Corinthians 1:3–5; Galatians 6:2), and grow in love for love's sake (Proverbs 3:3; 1 John 4:8, 19).

6

ONE BODY, MANY PARTS

Disability is best understood and responded to
in the context of community, especially one
in which the presence of God is felt keenly
and each individual is valued deeply.

—CHRIS RALSTON[1]

TAKEAWAY:
My church is incomplete without those who are affected
by disability and those who are suffering.

In this lesson, we focus on making disciples of all who believe in Jesus Christ. People who are disabled and marginalized often feel they have nothing to offer or they don't belong—even in the church. But God's spiritual gifts are for all people, without exception and regardless of abilities. In 1 Corinthians 12:22 the apostle Paul describes the church as one body with many parts. He goes a step further saying the church is incomplete when it fails to include those "parts of the body that seem weakest and least important [because they] are actually the most necessary" (NLT).

****

On your own, read the article below until you get to the reflection question. Think about your answer, or write it down. When everyone is ready, share with the group if you like.

Lesson

HARD TIMES IN THE WORLD

A Place to Belong

Emily Colson recalls the many years she and her son Max lived in isolation. Sundays were especially difficult because they couldn't find a place to fit in at church. Max struggled to communicate and control his behavior due to his autism. Autism is one of the fastest growing disabilities among children. According to the Centers for Disease Control and Prevention, one in every fifty-nine children in the U.S. will be diagnosed with some form of autism.[2] But Max is much more than his diagnosis. He is a young man whose bright smile and resilient spirit can inspire perseverance. Eventually, Emily and Max found a church home where they not only felt welcomed, they became part of the family.

Emily, author of *Dancing with Max*, says Sundays are very different these days.

> Autism held us hostage. But it is not a bitter memory; it is the soil from which God grew a victory. When I cross that threshold now with Max it feels like holy ground. Max comes most Sundays to serve as a greeter, and at the Welcome Center, and as part of the clean-up team, otherwise known as the "Grunt Crew." Max has clearly been given one of the lesser-known spiritual gifts of vacuuming. But what has

changed Max's life is what has changed mine; he is loved. He belongs. He is indispensable. We have been back to church for twelve years now, and none of this has been easy; sitting quietly is not part of Max's skillset. But it's as if the whole church is learning to breathe a little deeper, and in that, we find there is enough room for everyone.[3]

Without God's grace, all of us were once disabled spiritually, unable to move into his kingdom, blind to his purposes and deaf to his voice. But since we've received God's grace, we can extend this grace to all who enter the church looking for a place to belong. Some may reject our witness, like one young man with bipolar disorder who said, "If God does exist, I don't think he can help me." When this happens, remember how God never gave up on you and recommit yourself to always show God's grace to those in need.

ATTITUDES THAT HINDER THE GOSPEL

Social norms are made-up ideas that may appear to be natural and obvious to those who accept them. They are choices made by people rather than laws of God or nature. The media helped establish many of today's societal misconceptions about the marginalized and disabled. For example, people using white canes or wheelchairs are frequently portrayed as homeless or crime victims. Movies like *Rain Man* and *Forrest Gump* use humor to mask the pity audiences feel for these men with autism. These social norms can result in attitudes that devalue and hurt people, even when we are unaware of our actions. Progress has been made over the past few years with more positive depictions of those with disabilities in shows such as *Parenthood*, *Speechless*, and *The Good Doctor*.

You may be wondering what social norms have to do with evangelism and discipleship in the church.

Leviticus 19:14 says, "You shall not curse the deaf or put a stumbling block before the blind, but you shall fear your God: I am the LORD." God makes it clear that he does not find humor in mocking people with disabilities, calling them names, or treating adults as if they were uneducated children. Even some well-meaning Christians have incorrectly labeled people with special needs as *holy innocents*, meaning they are incapable of sin or the results of sin. This suggests they may be punished enough for their sins by their sufferings. Another misconception suggests children and adults with special needs were dropped on earth to make us count our own blessings or give us opportunities for selfless service. This thinking disrespects people as objects to be used for our personal edification.

If we prejudge the faith of the disabled and marginalized, we may presume they are incapable of becoming Christians with spiritual gifts to share. Nothing could be further from the truth. Now that we're aware of these pitfalls, let's focus on a "WHOLE-istic" approach for including all people in the body of Christ.

NOTE: If you think you have hidden attitudes that may be hindering you from reaching out to friends with special needs, take a moment for silent prayer to confess these attitudes to God. Then move on to the reflection question.

REFLECTION QUESTION:

Our verse from Leviticus says, "You shall not curse the deaf or put a stumbling block before the blind, but you shall fear your God: I am the LORD" (19:14). This suggests that those who are unkind to people with disabilities will have to answer to God. What does this tell us about God? (List several insights.)

Once the group has compiled a list, continue with the lesson together.
Have someone read aloud.

Lesson

BIBLE FOUNDATION

A Truly Inclusive Church

People with disabilities are consistently ignored, excluded, or forgotten by most evangelistic outreaches. Unfortunately, disability ministry is frequently considered a caregiving service rather than a ministry committed to welcoming children and adults with special needs and sharing the gospel with them. This may require a fresh way of thinking about evangelism. People who grew up with a formula for sharing the gospel may need to learn to trust the Holy Spirit's work in each person's heart. This begins with prayerfully seeking new opportunities to build caring relationships.

What is salvation? Romans 10:9 says, "If you confess with your mouth that Jesus is Lord and believe in your heart that God raised him from the dead, you will be saved." And Jesus said, "I am the way, and the truth, and the life. No one comes to the Father except through me" (John 14:6). Salvation is through—and only through—Jesus Christ.

Thank God, our salvation isn't based on what we do or don't do, but rather on who Jesus is and what he has done. Our performance may go back and forth, but Jesus is always the same, saving us by grace and through faith (see Ephesians 2:8–9). Becoming a Christian and growing in Christ requires a commitment to him (see Mark 8:34–38).

One father who has the courage to trust God's eternal plan for his son is Doug Mazza, former president and COO of Joni and Friends. His son Ryan was born with severe facial and skull deformities caused by a rare chromosome condition, leaving him severely disabled. But Doug believes that people with developmental and intellectual disabilities often understand much more than they seem to comprehend.

> My son, who is now thirty-six years old, has never spoken a word to me, and the doctors say he has the intellect of a young child. Still, I have presented the entire gospel to him and asked him to receive Christ into his heart. I knew that as his father it was my responsibility, even though I had no way of knowing how much Ryan truly understood. It brought me great comfort as well. Did I need to take that step? Maybe not, but if I share the gospel with others, why would I not share it with my own son?[4]

Colossians 1:28 says, "Him we proclaim, warning everyone and teaching everyone with all wisdom, that we may present everyone mature in Christ." The gospel is for *everyone*.

Individuals with physical disabilities, such as a birth defect, disease, injury, stroke, or other conditions, have the same spiritual needs as those without disabilities. They may question God's sovereignty and need an accepting, supportive church to help them learn to trust God. Depending on their limitations, they may require accessible transportation and facilities or Christian materials adapted to meet their needs such as large-print Bibles and books, a sign language interpreter, or hands-on assistance.

As part of the body of Christ, we are all called to serve and to be served by others. Yet, many churches are missing an untapped well of volunteers—people with disabilities. Sadly, they are often overlooked for service. Some are just waiting to be invited to use their God-given gifts and talents.

Read 1 Corinthians 12:7–27 and then answer the discussion questions.

DISCUSSION QUESTIONS:

- Who gives spiritual gifts to believers?
- What is the purpose of spiritual gifts?
- What should our attitude be toward those whose spiritual gifts are different from our own?

By specifically naming the gifts, Paul emphasizes their diversity, equality, and unity. Our spiritual gifts are not to be used selfishly for personal gain, but for the benefit of unifying the church. Therefore, when some gifts are missing, the whole church community suffers.

Romans 12:4–8 says, "For as in one body we have many members, and the members do not all have the same function, so we, though many, are one body in Christ, and individually members one of another. Having gifts that differ according to the grace given to us, let us use them: if prophecy, in proportion to our faith; if service, in our serving; the one who teaches, in his teaching; the one who exhorts, in his exhortation; the one who contributes, in generosity; the one who leads, with zeal; the one who does acts of mercy, with cheerfulness."

God designed our human bodies with many functioning parts. Each one is essential to the task for which it was created and all of the parts are interdependent. In the metaphor of *the body*, Paul suggests there is no place for people who consider their spiritual gifts superior or more important than others' gifts. Those who seem weaker are actually indispensable, and the health of the body depends on their active exercise of each individual spiritual gift.

Lesson

THE°
WITNESS

Using Unique Vessels

We need to be aware of any biases and also leery of making assumptions. Individuals with disabilities should be asked about their interests and strengths just like any other potential volunteer. Sometimes church leaders automatically allocate the role of prayer ministry to people with limited mobility or visual impairments. This may be a mistake since it fails to consider that some of these friends may have excellent financial, organizational, or administrative skills that could provide a vital service to the church. They may be skilled artists, singers, musicians, designers, carpenters, or seamstresses. The same is true for people coping with hardships such as cancer or multiple sclerosis. They may be excellent youth workers or Sunday school teachers.

Even though Tyson and Paige Snedeker are both confined to wheelchairs and legally blind, they are each pursuing God with all their hearts. Tyson delves into Bible studies with the help of his nurse, and Paige wrote a children's book to help others learn to trust God.

This story is both heartbreaking and heartwarming as we see a family with twin boys and a girl who all developed an unidentified degenerative neurological disorder. Watch Video Six at joniandfriends. org/gospel-hard-times. Then discuss the questions.

DISCUSSION QUESTIONS:

Paige expresses a confidence that God has a purpose for her life and wants to use her struggles, what about you?

- How are you using your spiritual gifts to bless others?
- Is it more difficult for people experiencing adversity to have faith? Is it harder to witness when all is going well, or when life is a daily struggle? The answer is yes and no. People's afflictions and fears may cause them to question their faith or to seek God with greater fervor. It depends on whether they've felt nurtured or experienced rejection in their lives. In either case, Christians can make a tremendous difference in the trajectory of an individual's or a family's life if we are supportive and willing to share our own stories of overcoming struggles and learning to trust God.

Joni Eareckson Tada says it's her wheelchair that initiates many of her opportunities to share the gospel. "People don't expect me to be happy in this wheelchair," says Joni. "And it always evokes a curious look when I tell them I have a reason for smiling and singing and living. Then I add, 'Jesus has blessed me! By the way, that's your reason for living too?' Sure, it catches people off guard, sometimes delighting them, sometimes making them curious, and sometimes sending them running for the nearest exit. But one thing's for sure . . . it got them thinking."[5]

If you claim Jesus Christ as your Savior, you have a story to share—one only you can tell. You have unique gifts designed to build up the body of Christ and to be his witness in the world.

You might pray the following items as part of your closing time together:

- Lord, forgive me if I have withheld my spiritual gifts or used them selfishly.
- Lord, help me promote unity in my church so there will be no division in the body of Christ.
- Lord, help our church equip all believers to use their spiritual gifts for the greater good.
- Lord, help me see if I am letting pride be a barrier to allowing others to serve my needs and use their God-given gifts.

Use the action plan to stay involved with what you have learned until the next time the group meets. You will have a chance to report on how it went.

Lesson

ACTION PLAN

Mission Possible: Becoming God's Secret Agent

Your mission, should you choose to accept it, is to search out and reveal the spiritual gifts of three people. As always, should you be caught you will confess and celebrate the knowledge of these actions. This message will self-destruct in five seconds. Good luck!

These iconic opening lines (with some modifications) are from a television series later made into action movies. *Mission Impossible* featured a team of secret government agents known as the Impossible Missions Force. In each exciting episode, the force accomplished its risky mission—the good guys saved the day.

As Christians, we're called to join God's task force—the priesthood of believers (1 Peter 2:5). As priests, we minister to one another through natural and spiritual gifts. First Peter 4:10 emphasizes this mission. "As each has received a gift, use it to serve one another, as good stewards of God's varied grace."

- List three people you can connect with this week to talk about spiritual gifts—theirs and yours.

- Discuss the diversity of your gifts and how they might work together for the good of the church.

7

LIVING FOR CHRIST: JONI'S STORY

*As tools in the hands of a loving, all-wise,
sovereign God, these very struggles that cause us such
frustration, sadness, anxiety, and tears,
will bring back benefits to our lives a thousandfold.*

—JONI EARECKSON TADA[1]

TAKEAWAY:

In this lesson, we consider how we can honor God
and serve others through our suffering.

We've all read about people who have faced unimaginable affliction and pain but somehow continue to remain steadfast in their
Christian faith. Over the past few lessons, we've learned that no one
is immune from suffering in our world. We've also seen how God
can redeem our struggles for his purposes. Joni Eareckson Tada has
triumphed through tremendous adversity for more than fifty years
by trusting in God's redemptive plan and believing that his incredible
power rests upon her.

* * * *

On your own, read the article about Joni until you reach the reflection question. Think about your answer, or write something down, and be prepared to share your thoughts once the group is ready.

Lesson

**HARD TIMES
IN THE
WORLD**

God's Plan for Our Suffering

In 2017, Joni Eareckson Tada celebrated fifty years of being in a wheelchair.

Before Joni's diving accident at age seventeen, she enjoyed riding horses through green pastures on her family's farm, gathering with friends around bonfires at the beach, and trying to keep up with her older sisters. It all changed with a devastating tragedy that left Joni paralyzed for life. "When I broke my neck, I felt as though God had walked into the room and upset the puzzle table," says Joni. "Not that I had everything figured out; it's just that before my accident, I figured my future would be a simple process of putting the puzzle pieces of my life together, all nice and orderly."

Joni realized that nothing bursts our bubble of expectation more quickly than a disability. She spent two painful years in rehabilitation, struggling with depression, loss, and her faith in God. She reflected back on those hard times during a recent chapel presentation at Grand Canyon University:

> You see, God's got his reasons for allowing so much pain and heartache and suffering, and those reasons are good and right and true. But I will be the first to tell you that when your

heart is being wrung out like a sponge, an orderly list of the sixteen good biblical reasons as to why this is happening, it can sting like salt in the wound. You don't stop the bleeding with the answers.

Oh yes, there comes a time when people stop asking "Why?" with a clenched fist and start asking "Why?" with a searching heart. And that's a great time for the Bible's answers. But when the suffering is fresh, answers don't always reach the problem where it hurts, and that's in the gut and in the heart.[2]

Trusted friends and family poured out God's love and mercy while pointing Joni back to the Word. She emerged from rehabilitation with new skills and a fresh determination to help others in similar situations. Joni learned to lean hard on God's grace in every situation. As a result, the word *paralyzed* hardly describes this vibrant woman who has founded a worldwide ministry, written fifty books, spoken in more than forty-five countries, and created stunning artwork with a paintbrush held between her teeth.

Like ripples in a pool of water, God has used Joni again and again. Whether it is a Bible teacher in Uganda, a death-row prisoner in Leavenworth, a retired physical therapist in Cuba, a boy with autism riding horseback in Texas, or an exhausted mother in Portugal, God continues to use Joni and the organization she founded to transform lives. And for this, Joni celebrates the faithfulness of God!

"Know therefore that the LORD your God is God, the faithful God who keeps covenant and steadfast love with those who love him and keep his commandments, to a thousand generations." (Deuteronomy 7:9)

PUSHING BACK THE DARKNESS

You may be thinking: Joni's life is inspiring, but I'm not Joni! Yes, but you are God's unique creation—and his special plan for you includes all of your struggles and weaknesses. In hard times, God's intention is not to frustrate us or confuse us; he promises to develop and refine us. "Count it all joy, my brothers, when you meet trials of various kinds, for you know that the testing of your faith produces steadfastness. And let steadfastness have its full effect, that you may be perfect and complete, lacking in nothing" (James 1:2–4).

Is there a crisis God has allowed in your life that could equip you to live for a cause greater than yourself? "God took what was once a crisis and birthed out of it a wonderful cause—the cause of the weak and needy, and I couldn't be more honored to do it," Joni says. "This is why my life's motto is Psalm 82:3, 'Defend the cause of the weak and fatherless; maintain the rights of the poor and oppressed' (NIV)."

In 1990, the National Council on Disability sent the Americans with Disabilities Act (ADA) to Congress. President George H. W. Bush signed it into law. Joni served as a member of the council under President Ronald Reagan and President Bush. She remembers the signing ceremony on the south lawn of the White House, especially for the words of the council's executive director, Paul Hearne, who said: "The ADA will mean that there will be mechanical lifts on buses and ramps into restaurants . . . open doors in places of employment. But this law will not change the hearts of the bus driver, restaurant owner or the employer." After a long pause and with wet eyes, Paul Hearne lifted his glass in a toast: "Here's to changed hearts."[3]

God's heart breaks for those whom society finds it easier to reject or marginalize—the poor, the orphan and widow, those with disabilities. He is the guardian and protector of those who are at a disadvantage. As Christians, he calls us to advocate on their behalf and "speak up for those who cannot speak for themselves" (Proverbs 31:8 NIV).

Bonnie is one of Joni's friends who, in spite of her own struggles, continues to push back the darkness. Joni says this about her friend:

> Bonnie is a polio-quadriplegic, who contracted polio back in the early '50s. She's one of the few polio quads still living. That's amazing given the many hardships she faces. One day Bonnie said to me: "You know, Joni, all of my polio friends have died and some have even given up on living before dying, but there is more for me to do and I want to do it." I love that attitude. Yes, a disability can make for a very hard life, but Bonnie will tell you that with the right attitude, even life with polio quadriplegia can be full of joy. It's the spirit of Romans 6:4 where it says, "Just as Christ was raised from the dead through the glory of the Father, we too may live a new life" (NIV). Bonnie will tell you that every day is a chance to experience life in Christ, new and fresh.[4]

It is only in the context of God's sovereignty that suffering has any purpose. Apart from a loving God, who uses suffering for his glory, our afflictions are meaningless. But in his hands, hard times can become a means of bringing others to faith in Jesus Christ.

REFLECTION QUESTION:

Consider the question posed earlier: Is there a crisis God has allowed in your life that could equip you to live for a cause greater than yourself? How might you answer?

After a time to think and share, have someone read aloud as you complete the rest of the lesson together, or take turns reading.

To discover a person's true nature, look at his friends.
The deepest friendships are forged in the fire of adversity.
When darkness besieges you, a true friend holds the light
at the end of the tunnel that beckons you forward.
In Proverbs 17:17 David described a friend as one
who "loves at all times." It may be humbling when your
friend sits in a wheelchair or mumbles his words.
Yet, his light is equally bright when Jesus Christ
shines through him.[5] —Pat Verbal

BIBLE
FOUNDATION

Walking in the Light

For human beings truly to be in relationship with God, we must choose to be. When we choose his light over darkness, it influences our attitudes and our ultimate outcomes.

In Genesis 37:23–24, a young Joseph finds himself in a deep pit at the hands of his own brothers and is sold into slavery. He later ends up in a dark Egyptian prison cell for a crime he didn't commit. We don't know if Joseph struggled to understand why his life kept spiraling downward, but he continued to trust God and honor him through his service to others. Eventually, he stands before his brothers as second in command of Egypt, proclaiming God's redemptive power: "As for you, you meant evil against me, but God meant it for good, to bring it about that many people should be kept alive, as they are today" (Genesis 50:20).

Like Bonnie and like Joseph, our journey through the darkness requires faith even when we cannot see the light and things don't make sense.

Luke tells about a time Jesus was teaching and healing:

> Some men were bringing on a bed a man who was para-
> lyzed, and they were seeking to bring him in and lay him
> before Jesus, but finding no way to bring him in, because

of the crowd, they went up on the roof and let him down with his bed through the tiles into the midst before Jesus. And when he saw their faith, he said, "Man, your sins are forgiven you." And the scribes and the Pharisees began to question, saying, "Who is this who speaks blasphemies? Who can forgive sins but God alone?" When Jesus perceived their thoughts, he answered them, "Why do you question in your hearts? Which is easier, to say, 'Your sins are forgiven you,' or to say, 'Rise and walk'? But that you may know that the Son of Man has authority on earth to forgive sins"—he said to the man who was paralyzed—"I say to you, rise, pick up your bed and go home." And immediately he rose up before them and picked up what he had been lying on and went home, glorifying God. And amazement seized them all, and they glorified God and were filled with awe, saying, "We have seen extraordinary things today." (Luke 5:18–26)

This man who was paralyzed had friends who trusted that Jesus was the Light and were willing to go the extra mile to make sure the man was in the right place at the right time. Imagine the darkness the man had lived with and the thrill of being let down through the roof. Jesus healed the man when he saw their faith, and used it as a lesson for the religious leaders who were more concerned with protocol. Their boldness on behalf of their friend provided an opportunity for God's glory to shine, and the man's life was forever changed.

Whether we're advocating for someone within our families, or as a friend or a caregiver, we must be aware that it puts us in the middle of a spiritual battle.

Ken Tada and Joni Eareckson fell in love and married in 1982, and have traveled the world together. Although Joni has others who help, Ken also serves as her caregiver. "I'm constantly aware that Joni and I are in the midst of a spiritual battle. The devil already hates

Christian marriage, and if a wife or a husband has a disability, Satan no doubt feels he's got the edge. But he's wrong! Second Corinthians 12:9 assures us that God's power has the edge when we are weak."[6]

Whether traveling or at home, Ken lovingly cares for Joni's needs, but he admits it was overwhelming in the early days. People often say that Joni makes disability seem normal, but Ken understands that it's not that simple. While he loves his wife and has never regretted his decision to marry Joni, that doesn't make it easy. Disability has a way of testing couples, but Ken shares what he's discovered is key:

> The secret of good caregiving is a constant awareness of one's desperate need of Jesus Christ; a steady reliance on him like breathing in and breathing out. The fact is, when I'm serving Joni, I'm serving Christ. Colossians 3:23 reminds every caregiver that no matter how difficult or demanding the routines, "Whatever you do, work at it with all your heart, as working for the Lord, not for human masters." When my focus is on Jesus, caregiving may feel extremely tiring, but the work doesn't have to be tiresome—it's for him. I may get weary, but life doesn't have to be wearisome—again, it's all for him and his glory. When I minister to Joni's needs, I'm serving the Savior.[7]

Joni and Ken Tada live their lives for others. They genuinely love people and encourage others to respond to Jesus. They are changing lives not in spite of, but because of their weaknesses. They are used by their Creator, about whom Isaiah says:

> He gives power to the faint,
>   and to him who has no might he increases strength.
> Even youths shall faint and be weary,
>   and young men shall fall exhausted;
> but they who wait for the LORD shall renew their strength;
>   they shall mount up with wings like eagles;

they shall run and not be weary;
  they shall walk and not faint. (Isaiah 40:29–31)

DISCUSSION QUESTIONS:

- When do you feel weak, or powerless, or tired?
- When darkness pushes in, what has helped you trust God for new strength?

Great leaders inspire greatness in all of us. Joni Eareckson Tada and her husband, Ken, are such leaders and friends to many along the journey of affliction and hardship. Has anyone in the group been a caregiver or advocate for a person in need? Would you like to tell about that?

**THE
WITNESS**

Jesus in the Darkness

Cancer is a word that can curdle the blood. In 2010, Joni was diagnosed with stage III invasive breast cancer, and underwent a mastectomy followed by five months of chemotherapy. At a low point, Joni broke down. "I can't do this," she said, sobbing in Ken's arms. "It's too much, too overwhelming. I can't do it." Joni knew she faced the battle of her life, but she also knew Jesus was still right by her side. With Jesus, there is always hope. He even believes your fight with cancer can be a good one (see 1 Timothy 6:12). In her first day of chemo, Joni began the prayerful habit of looking to God's Word for emotional balance as well as a healthy dose of encouragement.

In 2018, after being cancer-free for several years, doctors discovered a small nodule that had developed at the site of Joni's mastectomy. Her steadfast faith continues to inspire and encourage others.

> Cancer is like a big wall. You can sit at its base and spend hours studying its height and thickness, learning about who built it and how it was designed. Or you can spend hours learning how to scale the wall, to climb to the top to get a better vantage point on God. You can let cancer be like a sheepdog that snaps at your heels, driving you down the road to Calvary where you otherwise might not be inclined to go. As I've heard Dr. John Piper say, "Don't waste your cancer."

Of all the things in this world to waste, please do not waste your sufferings. They are a textbook that will teach you not only about yourself, but also about your great and compassionate God.[8]

Watch an update from Joni as she shares a little about the twists and turns along her cancer journey (Video Seven at joniandfriends.org/gospel-hard-times). Then discuss the questions below.

DISCUSSION QUESTIONS:

- Has someone in your family been impacted by cancer?
- When was a time that you wanted to ask God, "What are you doing?"
- What did Joni refer to as little splashovers of heaven?

NOTE: If you know someone battling cancer, they can find additional encouragement by watching more of Joni's story: "Cancer – Joni's Journey: Part 1 and 2" at www.joniandfriends.org/TV.

Cancer, divorce, disability, or financial crisis—all of these things seem to scatter the puzzle pieces of life and what we thought it would look like. It's natural to wonder how these things can be part of God's plan. As we've learned over the past few weeks, we can bring our questions to God. Joni shares this advice:

God has wired life to be difficult. Inconvenient and unwanted upheavals to our plans are part of what it means to live in a broken world. Personal growth means learning how to deal morally and compassionately with these interruptions. Change potentially stretches the soul. So, put the puzzle pieces away and fold up the puzzle table. God wants you to move beyond your urge to figure everything out and understand "how it all fits." Lean hard into his grace and you'll find that change isn't as scary as you thought.[9]

From oppression and violence he redeems their life,
and precious is their blood in his sight. (Psalm 72:14)

Lesson

PRAYER FOCUS

We rarely stop to consider the people whose lives we touch. As you spend time with the Lord today, ask him to bring those people to mind. Thank him for helping you be his witness and celebrate how he works through you to encourage others.

- Pray that when your way is dark and things don't make sense, your faith will still be a light to someone in need.
- Ask God to show you ways to serve people enduring hard times, especially those in your church. Look for ways to relieve human suffering by partnering with local compassion ministries.

Now use the action plan to stay involved with what you have learned, on your own, until the next time the group meets.

**ACTION
PLAN**

Ten Ways to Be a Light

People with disabilities often face a higher risk of being excluded in their churches and community, but you can make a difference! Here are ten easy ways for you to start reaching out to people affected by disability in your community:

1. If you are able-bodied, don't park in accessible parking spaces—not even for a moment.

2. Make an effort to include people with disabilities in church and community gatherings.

3. If you think assistance might be needed, don't hesitate to ask a person with disability how you might help. That person can tell you the easiest and safest way.

4. Ask your local library to increase their selection of large print books.

5. Spearhead a committee to raise funds for an elevator, ramp, or curb cut where it may be needed.

6. Hold the door open for a person using a wheelchair or crutches.

7. It may be difficult for parents of children with disabilities to find experienced babysitters, but they, too, need an evening out now and then. Offer to help!

8. Suggest that your church or organization take on a service project. You can rake lawns, do repair jobs, or wash windows for homeowners with disabilities in your area.

9. Make sure walkways and aisles are wide enough that a wheelchair can navigate freely.

10. Most importantly, just be friendly!

Don't just pretend to love others. Really love them. Hate what is wrong. Hold tightly to what is good. Love each other with genuine affection and take delight in honoring each other. (Romans 12:9–10 NLT)

8

REASONS FOR HOPE

Most of us see life as an arc beginning with birth,
which we can't remember, and death, which we can't
imagine. Jesus spoke of his role before birth
and after death and his years on earth as a period
of transition. That point of view changes everything.

—PHILIP YANCEY[1]

TAKEAWAY:

God's yes may look different from
our initial thoughts and prayers.

In this lesson, we celebrate our hope in Jesus Christ who died in our place and swung open the door to spiritual healing and eternal life. This is the good news of the gospel. Regardless of our abilities, fears, or weaknesses, our hope must be in "the living God, who is the Savior of all people, especially of those who believe" (1 Timothy 4:10). Even when our prayers seem to go unanswered, we can trust that God is working all things together for our good (see Romans 8:28).

* * * *

On your own, read the following article until you get to the reflection question. Think about your answer, or write it out.

Making All Things New

Mark is a twenty-five-year-old wheelchair user who admits that he often dreams about a planet exclusively for people with disabilities. In this magical place, there wouldn't be questions about who is normal or abnormal. No one would be labeled *handicapped* because everyone would have various limitations and abilities. There would be no name-calling, stares, or fears about trying new things. All prejudice would be replaced with genuine empathy. People would never have to suffer in silence. Mark would not be singled out to face limited opportunities in education, sports, employment, and social events. Everyone would be encouraged to reach his or her highest potential.

In the beginning, God gave us a perfect world without disabilities, pain, and suffering. When sin entered the world, everything changed. But God's prophets from Isaiah to Malachi promised all people a hope and a future. In the book of Revelation, the apostle John recounts a compelling vision of the new world to come: a place where God "will wipe away every tear from their eyes, and death shall be no more, neither shall there be mourning, nor crying, nor pain anymore, for the former things have passed away" (Revelation 21:4).

HOPE STEALERS

Throughout this study, we've met people in crises, hanging on by a thread and desperately crying out to God. Each one faced some giant "hope stealer." Their lives are vivid illustrations of Jesus's warning: "In the world you will have tribulation" (John 16:33).

While this verse has applied to adults for generations, it is increasingly true for today's youth. It's evident in popular programs like *13 Reasons Why* and *Pretty Little Liars*, which dramatize underage drinking, drugs, violence, sex, rape, and teen suicides. Even little children—like the ones Jesus set on his lap and blessed—are losing their innocence. Some are afraid to go to school after hearing about school shootings. Others are raised in overcrowded foster care systems. Many struggle with bullies, gangs, and growing anxieties.

The hope stealers in your life may not have been mentioned in these lessons, but you are intimately acquainted with them. Maybe their names are poverty, discontentment, obesity, pride, infertility, divorce, unemployment, or broken relationships? While you continue to fight off the struggles that try to derail you, they viciously regroup and strike again. But there is good news: you can defeat these repeat offenders. Jesus promised this in the second part of John 16:33 when he said, "But take heart; I have overcome the world."

Many people refer to suffering as hell on earth, and, in a sense, it is. But our suffering could be worse if it were not for the loving hand of God who limits suffering in our lives and the world. Hell is real, however, and those who reject Jesus, God's chosen Lamb, will face punishment. Jesus talked more about hell than he did heaven (see Matthew 8:11–12; 10:28; 13:49–50, Luke 16:19–31). Jesus wanted us to understand that sin—not suffering—is the real hope stealer.

REFLECTION QUESTION:

Identify and name a couple of your hope stealers.

Now complete the rest of the lesson together with someone reading the articles aloud, or group members taking turns.

Hope Builders

Hope flows when we learn to trust that God is always working for our good regardless of our circumstances, even when God's answers to our prayers seem to be "no" or "not yet." We can learn valuable lessons while we wait on God. Waiting has a way of building a solid foundation of unshakable hope in Christ Jesus.

Waiting on God Is a Hope Builder. "Wait for the LORD; be strong, and let your heart take courage; wait for the LORD!" (Psalm 27:14).

Brent Olstad has always had a strong dislike for waiting rooms. In his mind, waiting rooms are a prelude to bad news like when the dentist says you need a root canal or the auto mechanic says the car transmission is shot. Brent's aversion to waiting rooms grew stronger when his son Bryce was diagnosed with spina bifida.

"I remember how uncomfortable it felt to sit in a waiting room filled with strangers, hiding behind old magazines," says Brent. "Sometimes I would wonder what circumstances had brought them there, but mostly I fixated on my own problems. As time went on I found myself in other waiting rooms wondering if my son would live or die. I sat in straight-backed chairs, drinking old coffee from paper cups, and watching TV ads that claimed life would be great if I used a certain brand of toothpaste. Time seemed to stand still waiting for answers to countless questions."

Through the years, Brent discovered the art of meaningful waiting that has given him new hope. Today, he sees waiting rooms differently. "In waiting rooms, I have opportunity to commune with God and find peace in his presence," says Brent. "I can fulfill the needs of others who wait by listening and offering insights in casual conversation. I have opportunity to take stock and contemplate decisions. And while I'm not preoccupied with death, waiting rooms open my eyes to the fact that life is precious and it does end. But death is only a prelude to a wonderful new life with God where I picture my son running, jumping, and playing the trombone."[2]

God has a waiting room for us all. It is found under his wings of love and care.

Rejoicing Is a Hope Builder. "Through him we have also obtained access by faith into this grace in which we stand, and we rejoice in hope of the glory of God. Not only that, but we rejoice in our sufferings, knowing that suffering produces endurance, and endurance produces character, and character produces hope" (Romans 5:2–4).

In the flesh, rejoicing in suffering sounds a bit ridiculous. The secret is that we rejoice in the glory of God and the things it produces. What are the end results, according to the passage in Romans 5? List them below.

1.

2.

3.

These by-products allow us to accept suffering on God's terms. Those of us who joyfully endure and walk in godly character look to Jesus for assurance during agonizing pain or ongoing struggles. Does this make the pain go away or change our circumstances? Certainly not. Are there still days when we just can't seem to rally our resilience enough to rejoice? Probably. It does, however, make it possible to endure suffering and yet remain hopeful.

Staying on Mission Is a Hope Builder. "For the grace of God has appeared, bringing salvation for all people, training us to renounce ungodliness and worldly passions, and to live self-controlled, upright, and godly lives in the present age, waiting for our blessed hope, the appearing of the glory of our great God and Savior Jesus Christ, who gave himself for us to redeem us from all lawlessness and to purify for himself a people for his own possession who are zealous for good works. Declare these things; exhort and rebuke with all authority. Let no one disregard you" (Titus 2:11–15).

As Christians, we have a mission to witness, teach, and encourage believers to remain committed to the tenets of our faith. Joni says, "Over many years I have come to see a Christian's hope as the assurance that in the end, everything will be okay. Such hope is not based on your life getting better, or your pain going away, or your circumstances improving. Our hope is based on the Blessed Hope, Jesus Christ. In the end, Jesus will remove all pain, dry our tears, and take away our heartaches. When we can trust Jesus, we can persevere a little longer."

When we see friends and family give their lives to Jesus, our hope overflows. Although we still grieve the loss of those who die in Christ, our hope gets stronger and heaven gets sweeter. The cloud of witnesses in Hebrews 12 encourages us to look to Jesus, "the founder and perfecter of our faith, who for the joy that was set before him endured the cross . . . and is seated at the right hand of the throne of God" (vv. 1–2).

Trusting God's Promises Is a Hope Builder. "For all the promises of God find their Yes in him. That is why it is through him that we utter our Amen to God for his glory" (2 Corinthians 1:20).

Charles Spurgeon, England's best-known preacher in the mid-1800s, said this about God's promises: "In time of trouble, I like to find a promise which exactly fits my need, and then put my finger on it, and say, 'Lord, this is thy word: I beseech thee to prove that it is so, by carrying it out in my case.'"[3]

When we look to God's promises instead of our circumstances, we have a powerful prescription for holding on to hope. Even if the answer may be different from our initial thoughts or prayers, we must look for God's yes when we pray. God's promises also empower us to live out his plan so others might come to know him.

> Trust in the LORD with all your heart,
>   and do not lean on your own understanding.
> In all your ways acknowledge him,
>   and he will make straight your paths. (Proverbs 3:5–6)

DISCUSSION QUESTIONS:

- What or who has helped you find hope in times of need?
- When was the last time you clung to a promise from Scripture for yourself or a loved one?

THE WITNESS

Hope for the Future

The hope of heaven is an encouragement to Christian believers. The Bible is filled with word pictures of a glorious eternity God is planning for us. Isaiah describes it as a place where "the eyes of the blind shall be opened, and the ears of the deaf unstopped" (35:5). He says our joy will be everlasting; we'll find gladness and peace when "sorrow and sighing shall flee away" (35:10). What hope these Scriptures bring to all who face pain and suffering! However, our hope cannot be centered simply on our new and glorified bodies. It goes much deeper.

Brian Bushway's blindness helped him discover this truth. At fourteen, Brian's eyesight deteriorated suddenly, with no obvious cause. In a short time, he became totally blind. In the years that followed, Brian faced tough questions and challenges.

Because of his relationship with Jesus Christ and his desire to serve others, Brian now sees life in a whole new way. Watch Video Eight at joniandfriends.org/gospel-hard-times. Then discuss the questions below.

DISCUSSION QUESTIONS:

- Brian says, "Life is not about what we see and what we don't see. It's about what we do with ourselves while we're here." What does his statement have to do with his hope for the future?
- How do Joni's closing remarks apply to our hope of an eternity with Jesus?

Brian is living with a passion for eternity. God heard his cry for help and opened up a new world for him. Instead of waiting for a miracle to one day restore his sight, Brian says, "The miracle's already happened. I've already found Jesus." Brian sees with spiritual eyes, as do the other individuals we've met throughout our lessons.

How we face hard times depends on our perspective. The Bible repeatedly reminds us to live in the present with our future clearly in view. Every good thing on earth is a shadow of its fulfillment in heaven. The hope of heaven can fill us with joy even when the present is filled with pain or struggles. We can choose to live according to eternal values.

HOMEWARD BOUND

Someone has said: Life is hard, and then we die. Sure, it's a defeatist quote, but it is true; just incomplete. It's missing John's revelation of a new heaven and a new earth—a holy city on a hill where God will dwell with his people for eternity.

At the end of his Beatitudes, Jesus warned of the persecution and evil we will endure on earth. Then he gave this promise: "Rejoice and be glad, for your reward is great in heaven" (Matthew 5:12).

In his book *Applause from Heaven*, pastor Max Lucado asks this question: "When you look at this world, stained by innocent blood and smudged with selfishness, doesn't it make you want to go home?"[4]

Some say the term *home* has lost its meaning in our transient society.

But for the Christ-follower, home is an unconditional certainty—the bedrock of our faith. It's a place where prodigals are welcomed with open arms and where the Father says, "Well done, good and faithful servant" (Matthew 25:21). Lucado concludes his book with a contemporary picture of that great homecoming day.

> You may not have noticed it, but you are closer to home than ever before. Each moment is a step taken. Each breath is a page turned. Each day is a mile marked, a mountain climbed. You are closer to home than you've ever been. Before you know it, your appointed arrival time comes; you'll descend the ramp and enter the City. You'll see faces that are waiting for you. You'll hear your name spoken by those who love you. And maybe, just maybe—in the back, behind the crowds—the One who would rather die than live without you will remove his pierced hands from his heavenly robe . . . and applaud.[5]

Beloved, do not be surprised at the fiery trial when it comes upon you to test you, as though something strange were happening to you. But rejoice insofar as you share Christ's sufferings, that you may also rejoice and be glad when his glory is revealed. (1 Peter 4:12–13)

Here is Joni's prayer for us as we conclude this study:

> Dear God, we want to have a heavenly perspective, but it's
> hard to think about the joys of heaven when we face so many
> challenges. Please fill us with your Spirit. Give us your peace,
> the hope that can come only from you. Make us willing to
> trust you to meet our needs. Our sufferings give us a foretaste
> of what hell will be like, and we want to be used by you in
> ways that will make an eternal difference in people's lives.
> Thank you for the joy waiting for us in heaven. Help us to
> remember that what we face on earth isn't all there is. We
> look forward to being with you for eternity! In Jesus's pre-
> cious name we pray. Amen.

Use the action plan idea to stay involved with what you've learned
now that this study is over.

Lesson

ACTION PLAN

Hope in a Jar

Decorate a quart jar with a lid. Get as creative as you'd like. You can use colorful paint, a favorite fabric, or cut out pictures. On the front of the jar, write My Hope Jar or if you're doing it with your family, Our Hope Jar. Place small strips of paper and a pen near the jar to write notes that help you keep an eternal perspective. These could include:

- A Bible verse
- An answer to prayer
- A meaningful quote
- The title of a book or article
- A friend's testimony
- A story of God's protection or provision
- A special prayer request

If you're doing this as a family, children can draw a small picture that illustrates God's goodness. Some days you might add to the hope jar. Other days you may need to retrieve a slip of paper to keep your perspective on the things of God. We may not be citizens of heaven yet, but the hope jar will be a reminder of all that we have to look forward to as we live in Christ Jesus.

> But our citizenship is in heaven, and from it we await a Savior, the Lord Jesus Christ, who will transform our lowly body

to be like his glorious body, by the power that enables him even to subject all things to himself. (Philippians 3:20–21)

LEADER'S NOTES

LESSON 1: HARD TIMES, HARD QUESTIONS

GETTING STARTED
- ☐ Read the quote, the lesson's takeaway statement, and the introductory paragraph.

HARD TIMES IN THE WORLD

This section is intended to be a time for participants to read on their own and begin thinking about the reflection questions, coming together at that point to discuss what they have read. However, if your group includes people who struggle to read on their own, or if for other reasons you find it better to read this section aloud, you may choose to do so.

- ☐ Have participants read the article, "Facing the Unimaginable," on their own and think about the reflection questions or write some answers. When you sense the group is ready, ask for volunteers to share some of their reflections if they're comfortable doing so.

BIBLE FOUNDATION
- ☐ Begin reading "Our God Is Steadfast, Not Heartless."
- ☐ When you get to the verses from Job, ask participants to complete the exercise together as a group or individually, looking up each verse and identifying the different kinds of suffering.

We see all four basic kinds of suffering revealed through Job: physical, spiritual, emotional, and social.

Job 12:4 Social

Job 2:7–8, 12 Physical

Job 23:8–9, 15 Spiritual

Job 7:4, 13–14 Emotional

☐ Continue reading the Bible Foundation section and discuss the questions at the end.

THE WITNESS

The inclusion of the video clips and additional reflection questions in this section are optional, but are strongly recommended to help participants have a deeper connection to the lesson material.

☐ Begin reading "Good Can Come Out of Hard Times."
☐ View Video One at the link joniandfriends.org/gospel-hard-times.
☐ Read and ask participants to share their answers to the discussion questions as they feel comfortable.
☐ Read the remaining portion of "Good Can Come Out of Hard Times."

PRAYER FOCUS

Each week you may choose to close in prayer yourself or ask for a volunteer. Some group members may be reluctant to pray aloud this first week, but the goal is to get more participation as the weeks progress and attendees feel more at ease.

ACTION PLAN AND CLOSING

☐ Commend the action plan, "Grief Recovery," for participants to do at home. You might explain that it is not an assignment, but rather a way for them to remain involved with the material until the next time the group meets. If it helps, read some of the material to get members started.

☐ OPTIONAL: For this first lesson, consider inviting participants to give you written questions about hard times and the gospel. Use these submissions to pray for the group study and look ahead for lessons that may address these issues.

LESSON 2: JESUS IDENTIFIES WITH OUR SORROW

GETTING STARTED

☐ Ask about the previous lesson's action plan, and encourage a few group members to share their experiences.

☐ Read the quote and lesson's summary statement.

HARD TIMES IN THE WORLD

☐ Point out that the article, "Satan's War with the Kingdom of God," ends with an exercise that includes looking up several Bible passages. To save time, consider pairing participants up or dividing them into groups that will each take some of the passages to read and then share their answers with the group.

☐ Have participants read the article on their own, do the exercise, and think about the reflection questions or write some answers. When the group is ready, have participants report their findings from the Scripture exercise and share some of their reflections.

P = physical, SP = spiritual, E = emotional, or SO = social.

1. __E__ Jesus knew that his coming had caused the death of many baby boys in and around Bethlehem (Matthew 2:16–18).
2. __SP__ Jesus was tempted by Satan after forty days of fasting (Matthew 4:1–11).

3. _P/SO_ People believed that Jesus was a deceiver, and plotted against him (John 11:45–53; Matthew 12:14).

4. _SO_ The people of his hometown rejected him (Mark 6:1–6).

5. _P_ People tried to stone him (John 8:57–59; 10:31–39).

6. _E_ Jesus's heart ached over Jerusalem's terrible future (Matthew 23:37–39).

7. _SP_ Jesus was overwhelmed with sorrow and loneliness in Gethsemane (Matthew 26:38–40).

8. _SO_ Jesus was abandoned by his disciples when the crowd came to him in Gethsemane (Matthew 26:47–56).

9. _E/SO_ False witnesses accused him during his trial (Matthew 26:60).

10. _P_ Despite his innocence, Jesus was spat on, struck with fists, slapped, beaten, and mocked (Matthew 26:67–68; 27:30–31).

11. _P_ Roman soldiers crucified Jesus (Matthew 27:32–35).

12. _SP_ Jesus was separated from his Father because of the sin of the world that he bore for our sake (Matthew 27:45–46).

BIBLE FOUNDATION

NOTE: The tension between good and evil becomes increasingly more personal in the face of suffering. While this lesson acknowledges the evil work of Satan in the world, your goal is to help focus the discussion on the sovereignty of God in Jesus's earthly life. The suffering of our perfect Leader cleared the path for our salvation. And only in our own sufferings can we truly begin to appreciate the full extent of this precious gift—sufficient grace over our weaknesses here and for all eternity (2 Corinthians 12:9). Explain to the group that sympathy is an expression of sorrow for another person's suffering. Empathy, on the other hand, looks through the eyes of common experience and puts us in the other person's shoes.

☐ Begin reading "Jesus Understands Suffering."

☐ Ask a volunteer to read Hebrews 2:14–18.
☐ Talk about the discussion question.
☐ Continue reading about what Jesus accomplished for us through his suffering.

THE WITNESS

☐ Begin reading "Praying Through Suffering."
☐ View Video Two at the link joniandfriends.org/gospel-hard -times.
☐ Read and ask participants to share their answers to the discussion questions as they feel comfortable.
☐ Continue reading with "Redemption in the Face of Suffering."

PRAYER FOCUS

☐ Lead in prayer or ask for a volunteer.

ACTION PLAN

☐ Introduce the action plan, "Hidden Sorrows of the Heart," for participants to do at home.
☐ Discuss using a prayer journal. If you have used written prayers, consider sharing one with the group. If time allows, you might encourage participants to begin writing a brief prayer while the group is still gathered. Be sure to provide paper and pens.

LESSON 3: AN EVER-PRESENT HELP

GETTING STARTED

☐ Ask about the action plan from the last lesson, and encourage some participants to share their experiences.

☐ Read the quote and this lesson's summary statement.

HARD TIMES IN THE WORLD

☐ Have participants read the article, "The Promises of the Shepherd," on their own until they get to the reflection questions. Encourage them to write out some thoughts if it helps them. When the group is ready, allow time for members to share some of their reflections.

BIBLE FOUNDATION

NOTE: The point of this Bible discussion is twofold: (1) to illustrate God's goodness as the One who knows us and fights to protect us from all harm and (2) to highlight God's plan to use us to shepherd those who are lost. In hard times, we tend to focus on our own needs and fail to see that helping others can be part of our healing. This is evident in organizations such as Alcoholics Anonymous where people share their personal journeys to encourage the resolve of others, and in doing so they too receive new strength.

☐ Begin reading "The Goodness of the Shepherd."

☐ Discuss the questions at the end of the article.

THE WITNESS

☐ Begin reading "A Call to Feed God's Sheep."

☐ View Video Three at the link joniandfriends.org/gospel-hard -times.

☐ Read and ask members to share their answers to the discussion questions as they feel comfortable.

PRAYER FOCUS

- ☐ You may choose to close in prayer yourself or ask for a volunteer.
- ☐ Consider praying the words of Psalm 119:175–76, or asking a volunteer to do so.
- ☐ The writing exercise can be an aid to prayer. If time allows, encourage participants to write and/or share their memories of a time the Good Shepherd provided for them.

ACTION PLAN AND CLOSING

- ☐ Point out the "Seeking the Shepherd" activities. You may want to being reading the descriptions or explaining them. Encourage participants to commit to one of the activities in the coming week, or suggest another activity that helps them practice the presence of God.

LESSON 4: A PLACE OF HEALING

GETTING STARTED

- ☐ Ask about the previous lesson's action plan. Encourage a few group members to share their experiences in seeking the Good Shepherd.
- ☐ Read the quote, the lesson's takeaway statement, and the introductory paragraph.

HARD TIMES IN THE WORLD

NOTE: Some group members may have a strong emotional reaction to this story about attempted suicide due to experiences with family or friends. As a leader, you need to find a balance between being a sympathetic listener and keeping the lesson focused. If someone dominates the discussion or needs additional support, offer to meet with him or her after the session or encourage a visit with the pastor. You may want to provide the following additional statistics about suicide with your group: According to the National Center for Health Statistics, 575,000 people visited hospitals in 2015 for self-inflicted injuries. The total number of deaths due to suicide was 44,193, or 13.9 out of every 100,000 Americans.[1]

- ☐ Have participants read the article, "Living on the Edge," on their own and think about the reflection questions or write some answers. Discuss their reflections when the group is ready. Since this is their fourth lesson together, group members may be more open to sharing, but proceed with caution as this is a sensitive and highly personal topic.

BIBLE FOUNDATION

NOTE: A good Bible study presents the Word of God as a practical, living truth that informs how we are to think and interact in the world. While this is possible without the church, it is likely to be less effective and sustainable. Contrary to some beliefs, the church does not demand conformity. The New Testament church enjoyed diversity: Jews, Gentiles, Samaritans, the wealthy, and the poor. If you have people in your group who think the Christian life can be lived apart from the church, ask them to consider Christ's call in John 17:20–21 to be "one in the world" as a call for a healthy interdependence that empowers diversity in the church.

☐ Begin reading "The Church as a Healing Place."
☐ Allow time for participants to consider the checkboxes. You might want to let some share their responses.
☐ Continue reading the Bible Foundation section and discuss the question at the end.

THE WITNESS

☐ Begin reading "Open Doors, Open Hearts."
☐ View Video Four at the link joniandfriends.org/gospel-hard -times.
☐ Read and ask members to share their answers to the discussion questions as they feel comfortable.
☐ Continue reading or ask a volunteer to read the rest of this section.

PRAYER FOCUS

☐ Close in prayer or ask for a volunteer. Include prayers that group members would notice people who need comforting this week and might be of comfort to them.
☐ Consider the exercise where each member of the group writes the names of three people who need God's comfort and healing. You can pray for them individually or, where it's appropriate to share the names, in the group.

ACTION PLAN AND CLOSING

☐ Review the action plan and encourage participants to start thinking about it. If time allows and the group seems willing, read through it and briefly discuss what it asks.

LESSON 5: BRING IN THE BROKEN

GETTING STARTED

- ☐ Ask if anyone wants to share about a way they reached out to someone, or something they learned about their church's compassion ministries, from the last lesson's action plan.
- ☐ Read the quote, the lesson's takeaway statement, and the introductory paragraph.

HARD TIMES IN THE WORLD

- ☐ Have participants read the article, "Jesus, Open Our Eyes." Once everyone has gotten to the reflection questions, allow group members to share some of their thoughts. NOTE: In Luke 14, the Jewish leaders had the message of God's kingdom backwards. They sought honor and esteem and wanted to rule over the people. However, Jesus came to humble the proud and honor the lowly. He showed compassion for the outcasts and sinners, revealing the true character of God.
- ☐ Some members of your group may be represented in the statistics mentioned near the beginning of the article. If so, you may want to ask them to share some of their experiences.

BIBLE FOUNDATION

NOTE: The purpose of this lesson is to create a fresh awareness of the hurting people we see every day. As the leader, you are not merely the travel agent who gives out information—you're the tour guide. A tour guide goes on the journey, pointing out places of interest along the way. In group discussions, focus on these three markers: (1) Jesus's posture toward broken people, (2) the local church's welcome and inclusion of hurting families, and (3) our mission and calling to serve struggling adults and children, introducing them to our Savior, Jesus Christ.

☐ Read "Examine Our Hearts" aloud, or have some other reader or several readers do it.

☐ Discuss the exercise at the end of the section. Various group members will likely think of different ways to fill in the blanks. Encourage a variety of ideas.

THE WITNESS

☐ Begin reading "Friendship Evangelism."

☐ View Video Five at the link joniandfriends.org/gospel-hard -times.

☐ Read the discussion questions and ask participants to share their thoughts.

☐ Finish reading the section and the closing verse.

PRAYER FOCUS

☐ Lead in prayer or ask for volunteers. The insights gleaned from the Bible verse exercise at the end of the Bible Foundation section would make goods items for prayer, as do the prayer suggestions listed in the lesson.

ACTION PLAN

☐ "Meeting the Needs" introduces several ways group members might get involved with their church's compassion ministries. If you think it will be helpful, go over these suggestions as you encourage participants to take action in the coming week.

LESSON 6: ONE BODY, MANY PARTS

NOTE: This lesson is designed to challenge your group's understanding of the church. While the Scripture discussions may seem basic to the faith, ideas about a fully-inclusive church and the giftedness of people with disabilities may be new. Churches that truly function as the whole body of Christ grow deeper—not just larger in attendance. Help your group honestly evaluate how your church is doing in this area. Use the action plan to spark a roaring fire of passion. Joni Eareckson Tada describes this picture as "the church with its sleeves rolled up."

GETTING STARTED

- ☐ Ask about last time's action plan. Did anyone take any steps toward getting involved with their church's compassion ministries, and would like to tell about it?
- ☐ Read this lesson's opening quote, takeaway statement, and introduction.

HARD TIMES IN THE WORLD

- ☐ On their own, have participants read the article, "A Place to Belong." When they get to the reflection question, provide a time for them to share their thoughts.

BIBLE FOUNDATION

NOTE: This section briefly defines the gospel. Approach it prayerfully because someone in the group may be undecided about his or her faith in Jesus Christ. For more on how to share the gospel, see "The Good News" at www.joniandfriends.org/good-news/.

- ☐ Begin reading "A Truly Inclusive Church."
- ☐ When you get to the instructions to read 1 Corinthians 12:7–27, have someone find it in their Bible and read it aloud.

☐ Discuss the questions.

☐ Finish reading the section.

THE WITNESS

☐ Begin reading "Using Unique Vessels."

☐ View Video Six at the link joniandfriends.org/gospel-hard -times.

☐ Read and ask members to share their answers to the Discussion Questions as they feel comfortable.

☐ Read the rest of the article.

PRAYER FOCUS

☐ The prayer suggestions in the lesson include both prayers for the church and several personal prayers for forgiveness, insight, and godliness. Today might be a good day to encourage many group members to pray aloud, as they feel led.

ACTION PLAN

☐ Suggest that group members look at the action plan and begin planning to do it. TIP: You might want to ask the group to pair up into teams of two. Partners can keep each other accountable to complete the plan, and can begin by planning to discuss spiritual gifts with each other.

LESSON 7: LIVING FOR CHRIST: JONI'S STORY

GETTING STARTED

- ☐ Ask if anyone discussed spiritual gifts with someone else as part of the last lesson's action plan, and would like to share about the experience.
- ☐ Read this lesson's opening quote, takeaway statement, and introduction.

HARD TIMES IN THE WORLD

- ☐ Consider an opening activity before starting this section: Dump a box of puzzle pieces on the table or floor. Invite members of the study to pick up a puzzle piece to represent their current struggles or things in their lives that they don't have figured out. Some may pick up a handful. Ask a few to share one or two "life puzzles" that confound them.
- ☐ Have participants read the article, "God's Plan for Our Suffering," on their own and think about the reflection question. When the group seems ready, give an opportunity for some to share their responses.

BIBLE FOUNDATION

- ☐ If you think some participants may be unfamiliar with the story of Joseph, you might want to briefly summarize his life (Genesis 37—47) before the group gets started on this part of the lesson.
- ☐ Begin reading "Walking in the Light" and discuss the questions at the end of the section.

THE WITNESS

- ☐ Begin reading "Jesus in the Darkness."
- ☐ View Video Seven at the link joniandfriends.org/gospel-hard -times.

☐ Read and ask participants to share their answers to the discussion questions as they feel comfortable.

☐ Read the remaining portion of "Jesus in the Darkness."

PRAYER FOCUS

☐ Ask God to show you ways to serve people enduring hard times, especially those in your church. Look for ways to relieve human suffering by partnering with local mission organizations.

ACTION PLAN

☐ Commend the "Ten Ways to Be a Light" to the group, as a way to stay involved with the lesson until the next time you meet. Encourage members to select a few ideas from the list.

LESSON 8 – REASONS FOR HOPE

NOTE: The word *educate* means to "lead forth," which has been the goal of this study. If you think of these lessons as a road trip and each topic as a mile marker, some in your group may have altered their direction.

In lessons 1–3, your group identified past and present troubles in their lives. They were encouraged to yield to their fellow-sufferer, Jesus Christ, and discover how he is ever-present on their journey through afflictions and suffering.

In lessons 4–6, they found comfort and healing in serving others— broken sojourners with spiritual gifts and talents that could enrich their lives and the church.

And in lessons 7 and 8, you met others who are living by faith, clinging to hope, and yearning for our heavenly home.

As you pray for your group this week, consider the growth you've seen in the lives of those in your group. You might invite them to share the steps of faith they've witnessed in one another.

GETTING STARTED

☐ Ask if anyone has a story to share or some other report from the last lesson's action plan.

☐ Read this lesson's quote, takeaway statement, and opening paragraph.

HARD TIMES IN THE WORLD

NOTE: While some group members may welcome a lesson on hope and heaven, others may feel unworthy or unsure of their eternal home. Ask God to guide the discussions.

☐ Have group members read the article, "Making All Things New," on their own, stopping after they've had a chance to think about the reflection question. Provide a chance for some to share about their personal hope stealers.

BIBLE FOUNDATION

☐ Begin reading "Hope Builders."

☐ When you reach the exercise based on Romans 5:2–4, stop to allow the group to find and enter the right words from the passage.

1. Endurance
2. Character
3. Hope

☐ Read through the rest of the "Hope Builders" article until you reach the questions. Pause there for discussion.

THE WITNESS

☐ Begin reading "Hope for the Future."

☐ View Video Eight at joniandfriends.org/gospel-hard-times.

☐ Discuss the questions that follow the video.

☐ Continue reading to the end of the section.

PRAYER FOCUS

☐ As part of your closing time and prayer, thank God for the relationships that were built during this study. Encourage people to continue to stay in touch and pray for one another. Suggest that they pray Joni's closing prayer every day for a month. Consider a follow-up group social at the end of the month where they can invite someone they've witnessed to or encouraged as a result of the study. In this way, you'll be keeping hope alive!

☐ Ask a volunteer to close with Joni's prayer, or lead in prayer yourself:

ACTION PLAN

☐ If you have time and brought supplies, you might encourage participants to start working on the action plan before they leave.

ENDNOTES

FOREWORD

1. C. S. Lewis, *The Problem of Pain* (New York: Macmillan, 1947), 81.

LESSON 1: HARD TIMES, HARD QUESTIONS

1. John Piper and Justin Taylor, editors, *Suffering and the Sovereignty of God* (Wheaton, IL: Crossway Book, 2006), 209.

2. David Crowder Band, "How He Loves," by John Mark McMillan, track 10 on *Church Music*, sixstepsrecords, 2009.

3. Doug Mazza and Steve Bundy, *Another Kind of Courage: God's Design for Fathers of Families Affected by Disability* (Agoura Hills, CA: Joni and Friends, 2014), 55–57.

4. "Childhood Cancer Statistics," CureSearch for Children's Cancer, https://curesearch.org/Childhood-Cancer-Statistics.

5. Larry Waters, "The Problem of Evil and Suffering," *Beyond Suffering: A Christian View on Disability Ministry Course Reader* (Agoura Hills, CA: Joni and Friends, 2011). Waters was a former associate professor of Bible at Dallas Theological Seminary.

6. Joni Eareckson Tada and Steve Bundy with Pat Verbal, *Beyond Suffering: A Christian View on Disability Ministry Study Guide* (Agoura Hills, CA: Joni and Friends, 2011), 92.

7. Elisabeth Kübler-Ross, *On Death and Dying: What the Dying Have to Teach Doctors, Nurses, Clergy and Their Own Families* (New York: Simon & Schuster, Inc., 1969). For a Christian perspective on her work from the Biblical Counseling Coalition, see https://biblical counselingcoalition.org/2011/09/07/a-biblical-model-of-grieving-hope-in-the-midst-of-your-grief/.

LESSON 2: JESUS IDENTIFIES WITH OUR SORROW

1. Joni Eareckson Tada, *Hope . . . the Best of Things* (Wheaton, IL: Crossway Books, 2008), 20.

2. Brittney Martin, "Pass Through the Waters," *Christianity Today*, July/August 2018, 32.

3. The Barna Group, "Most American Christians Do Not Believe that Satan or the Holy Spirit Exist," Barna Group Research Releases, April 13, 2009, https://www.barna.com/research/most-american-christians-do-not-believe-that-satan-or-the-holy-spirit-exist/.

4. Martin, "Pass Through the Waters," 41.

5. David Lyons and Linda Lyons Richardson, "Praying in the Face of Pain," *Beyond Suffering: A Christian View on Disability Ministry Course Reader* (Agoura Hills, CA: Joni and Friends, 2011).

LESSON 3: AN EVER-PRESENT HELP

1. James Dobson compiled by Sarah Peterson, *In the Arms of God: Comforting Words from When God Doesn't Make Sense* (Wheaton, IL: Tyndale House Publishers, 1997).

2. Anne Graham Lotz, "Fixing My Eyes on Jesus," Proverbs 31 Ministries daily devotions, November 5, 2018, https://proverbs31.org/read/devotions/full-post/2018/11/05/fixing-my-eyes-on-jesus. The hymn quoted is "Trust Him When Thy Wants Are Many" by Lucy A. Bennett (1850–1927).

3. Jayne O'Donnell and Anne Saker, "Teen Suicide Is Soaring. Do Spotty Mental Health and Addiction Treatment Share Blame?" the website of *USA TODAY*, March 19, 2018, https://www.usatoday.com/story/news/politics/2018/03/19/teen-suicide-soaring-do-spotty-mental-health-and-addiction-treatment-share-blame/428148002/.

THE GOSPEL IN HARD TIMES

4. To learn more about the Joni and Friends internship program, visit www.joniandfriends.org/cause-4-life.

LESSON 4: A PLACE OF HEALING

1. Brennan Manning, *The Relentless Tenderness of Jesus* (Grand Rapids, MI: Fleming H. Revell, 2004), 68.

2. Joni Eareckson Tada, *A Place of Healing: Wrestling with the Mysteries of Suffering, Pain, and God's Sovereignty* (Colorado Springs, CO: David C. Cook, 2010), 41–42.

3. Billy Graham, *Hope for the Troubled Heart: Finding God in the Midst of Pain* (New York: Bantam, 1993), 143.

LESSON 5: BRING IN THE BROKEN

1. Francis Chan with Mark Beuving, *Multiply: Disciples Making Disciples* (Colorado Springs, CO: David C. Cook, 2012), 61.

2. "Nearly 1 in 5 People Have a Disability in the U.S., Census Bureau Reports," United States Census Bureau, July 25, 2012, https://www.census.gov/newsroom/releases/archives/miscellaneous/cb12-134.html.

3. Michael Yaconelli, *Dangerous Wonder* (Colorado Springs, CO: NavPress, 2003), 143.

4. Joni Eareckson Tada and Steve Bundy with Pat Verbal, *Beyond Suffering: A Christian View on Disability Ministry Study Guide* (Agoura Hills, CA: Joni and Friends, 2011), 191.

LESSON 6: ONE BODY, MANY PARTS

1. D. Christopher Ralston, "Editorial," *The Journal of the Christian Institute on Disability* 7.1 (Spring/Summer 2018): 9.

2. "What Is Autism?" Autism Speaks, https://www.autismspeaks.org/what-autism.

3. Emily Colson, "What Happens When You Yell at Church?" blog post July 1, 2016, https://www.emilycolson.com.

4. Joni and Friends, *Real Families, Real Needs: A Compassionate Guide for Families Living with Disability* (Carol Stream, IL: A Focus on the Family book published by Tyndale House, 2017), 39.

5. Joni Eareckson Tada and Steve Bundy with Pat Verbal, *Beyond Suffering: For the Next Generation* (Agoura Hills, CA: Joni and Friends, 2015), 209.

LESSON 7: LIVING FOR CHRIST: JONI'S STORY

1. Joni Eareckson Tada, *A Place of Healing: Wrestling with the Mysteries of Suffering, Pain, and God's Sovereignty* (Colorado Springs, CO: David C. Cook, 2010), 202.

.2. Joni Eareckson Tada quoted by Rick Vacek, "Tada Delivers a Moving Call to Action at Chapel" *GCU Today* (September 18, 2018) https://news.gcu.edu/2018/09/tada-delivers-a-moving-call-to-action-at-chapel/.

3. Joni Eareckson Tada and Nigel M. de S. Cameron, *How to Be a Christian in a Brave New World* (Grand Rapids, MI: Zondervan, 2006), 82.

4. "Bonnie Wants to Live," *Joni and Friends* radio, December 11, 2011, https://www.joniandfriends.org/radio/1-minute/bonnie-wants-live/.

5. Joni Eareckson Tada and Steve Bundy with Pat Verbal, *Beyond Suffering: A Christian View on Disability Ministry Study Guide* (Agoura Hills, CA: Joni and Friends, 2011), 186.

6. Ken Tada, "Caregiving: A Cause for Christ," *Beyond Suffering: A Christian View on Disability Ministry Course Reader* (Agoura Hills, CA: Joni and Friends, 2011).

7. Ibid.

8. Joni Eareckson Tada, *Diagnosed with Breast Cancer: Life After Shock* (Greensboro, NC: New Growth Press, 2012), 12–13.

9. Joni and Friends, *Real Families, Real Needs: A Compassionate Guide for Families Living with Disability* (Carol Stream, IL: A Focus on the Family book published by Tyndale House, 2017), ix–xi.

LESSON 8: REASONS FOR HOPE

1. Philip Yancey, *Rumors of Another World* (Grand Rapids, MI: Zondervan, 2003), 242.

2. Doug Mazza and Steve Bundy, *Another Kind of Courage: God's Design for Fathers of Families Affected by Disability* (Agoura Hills, CA: Joni and Friends, 2014), 37–37; 43–44.

3. Charles Spurgeon quoted by Joni Eareckson Tada, "Prescription of Promises," *Joni and Friends* radio, June 11, 2018, https://www.joniandfriends.org/radio/1-minute/prescription-promises/.

4. Max Lucado, *The Applause of Heaven* (Dallas, TX: Word Publishing, 1990), 188–90.

5. Ibid.

LEADER'S NOTES

1. "Suicide and Self-Inflicted Injury," Centers for Disease Control and Prevention (CDC), National Center for Health Statistics, https://www.cdc.gov/nchs/fastats/suicide.htm.

Nearly 1 billion people around the world live with disabilities.

For the past forty years, our programs and outreaches around the world have presented the hope of the gospel to individuals and families of individuals affected by disability. We energize the church, moving people from lack of awareness to including everyone into the fabric of worship, fellowship, and outreach. We also train and mentor people with disabilities to exercise their gifts of leadership and service in their churches and communities.

Joni and Friends' Mission
To communicate the gospel and equip Christ-honoring churches worldwide to evangelize and disciple people affected by disabilities.

To learn more about Joni and Friends, please visit
joniandfriends.org